A School Called Earth

By

Luis Miguel Falcao

Johannesburg, South Africa.
First Edition 2007

A School Called Earth

By Luis Miguel Falcao

Published by Zulu Planet Publishers
PO Box 91344 Auckland Park,
Johannesburg, 2006,
South Africa.

ZULU PLANET PUBLISHERS

First Edition 2007

© L.M. Falcao 2007

All rights reserved.
No part of this books may be copied, reproduced, recorded, broadcast, transmitted or stored in any way or manner, by any means or by any technology, in existence now or in the future, without prior written permission from the publisher.

Printed in Mauritius by Book Printing Services Ltd.

ISBN: 1-920153-03-05
ISBN13: 978-1-920153-05-2

CONTENTS

I. Prologue
II. Dedication
III. Foreword
IV. Author's Note

Chapter 1. The First tough lesson
    Meeting my Guide
    Meeting my biggest Critic

Chapter 2. The Creator
    God the Creator
    The Holy Trinity
    Continuous Growth

Chapter 3. How It All Works - Life On The Other Side
    What are you? Your Soul
    How is a Soul born?
    What happens when we die?
    Soul Families and group structures
    Playgrounds and Soul activities
    Soul roles
    Soul Roles explained
    Untimely Passing and Helping Themes
    Suicide – Is there Punishment?
    Past lives – why can't we remember?
    Cruel lives, traumatic death situations – why do we need to suffer?
    A Soulmate – does everyone have one?
    Animal Souls

      Do we up-grade from animals?
      Can we incarnate as animals?
      Can animal Souls become human?
      Picking a life and a body for this journey
      Life paths – The Lessons and Free Will

Chapter 4. Soul Advancement
      Soul Stages
            Stage 1: Baby Soul
            Stage 2: Young Soul
            Stage 3: Mature Soul
            Stage 4: Old Soul
            Stage 5: Advanced Soul
            A New Stage: Indigos

Chapter 5: Spirit Guides, Spirits, Ghosts and Angels
      What is a Spirit Guide?
      Primary Guides
      Secondary Guides
      Master Guides
      Do we know our Guides?
      Spirits and Ghosts
      Angels
      Earth Angels

Chapter 6: Why Earth – a really tough school
      Life Paths – The Lessons and Free Will

Chapter 7: Case Studies – the proof you have been waiting for.

Appendix: Janet's Letter to Luis

I. PROLOGUE

In the early hours of that June winter, my bedroom was freezing and outside it must have been close to zero degrees Celsius. I had woken with a familiar scent in the room and I knew that in a few moments I would again have an extraordinary visitor, called Uriall. The house was dark and asleep, not a single sound could be heard, yet in a few moments my room would light up like the sun though no one in the house would wake up or be disturbed. It was always like this. The worst that could happen would be some teasing in the morning by my mother and sisters because "Luis was talking in his sleep again".

I was nine years old and I really hated the world and all the people who lived in it, but this visitor was different. He had no hatred and no prejudice and he made me feel like I was important enough to warrant his undivided attention. The only annoying thing was that he never remembered my name and he always addressed me by what sounded like my second name Miguel. If you are wondering why I said always, it is because he had visited me in this way for as long as I could remember - and I can remember being born! Unbeknown to me, the visit this particular winter morning would be different to any other visit I had ever experienced, and one that I will never forget as long as I exist.

"Michaelilu" he called and "Yes, Lord" I answered (because I had read the passage on Joseph in the Bible and that's how he had answered). "Michaelilu, what is it that you want". Wow, I thought, my own genie in a brightly lit bottle as my mind scrambled for something important to ask for, including a car for my parents and a bike for myself so I wouldn't have to walk to school everyday. It felt like an eternity as I thought of the consequences of a futile request, but eventually I settled on what I thought was a ten out of ten answer. "I want to be wise. So wise that I know everything and so that I become so clever that my wisdom can help everyone in the world. That way they will all like me and that way no one will ever say that people like me are stupid".

I waited anxiously to see if he produced a magic wand, but instead the magnificent white light that surrounded him disappeared as if someone switched off the sun and, in the darkness, the shadow of a man was left. I felt afraid, really afraid, because I loved these visits, and now I felt as if my whole universe had collapsed because I had said something stupid and ruined the friendship. Now there was a grown man in my dark room and I wondered what hurt he was about to dish out.

Uriall slowly walked up to the edge of my bed, his footsteps making the wooden floorboards creak, and sat with his full weight on the edge of my mattress. "Michaelilu," he said, "I know that you are afraid, but you must not be. You and I are friends back home and I am here to help you. I know that this world is tough and very cruel to a young boy like you, but you are here for a special reason, and now that you have remembered why you are here I am ready to stand by you and help you until the time comes when you no longer need me. So, again, I ask you, Michaelilu, what is that you want, and are you sure that you want to help people, because the people who most need your help are also the people who are the cruelest to you?"

I put on the bravest voice I could and replied, "Yes, I do want to be wise so that I can help people, but can you please stop calling me Michaelilu, because my name is Luis!" "Luis is the name of your body, Michaelilu," he replied, "Michaelilu is your name back home. In time you will remember".

Chokma Michaelilu

Chokma Michaelilu: *"The Wisdom Of Michael"* (and the order of Michael) shared with the Saints.

Michael is the defender of the word. He insures the purity and the continuance of the Word in accordance with the Father's plan for our creation. His wisdom is given freely to the saints, and through his power he stands up on behalf of the righteous ones.

DR. J.J Hurtak, The Seventy-Two Sacred Names

II. Dedication

In memory of Justine

Thank-you to the Creator, Uriall, Mom and to all my friends who I love and who love me.

With a very special thanks to three Earth Angels, Gien, Mark and Sandrine for the painstaking hours taken to edit my Portuguese English. A loving smiling thanks to Michelle and Mary-Anne as this book was your idea.

And a very special bear-hugging thanks to Dr. David Lilley, you are my Guru.

To Deirdre, thanks for the journey. I will forever be grateful for the lessons that came with love.

And to you reading this book, may your Guides, Angels and the Holy Spirit of the Creator unfold your truth as you read on.

Without friends
A man has no family
With no family, all-purpose is hollow.

III. Foreword

Those of us who have become disillusioned with conventional religion and its prescriptions have turned to alternate sources to find and forge our spiritual path. This takes courage and insight, and not a small amount of curiosity. It is my considered opinion that if you are one such being, you will be reading this. Moreover, you would not be reading this if you were not meant to. . . .

In finding your own path you have, no doubt, encountered many teachings on spirituality, and may have made some of them your own. At the end of it, though, you have realised that each one is but a piece of the puzzle, one more step towards the meaning of life and our place in it.

This book makes sense. It takes many of those pieces of the puzzle and puts them together in a way that leads you to that "Ahh, so that's what it is," place of realisation. It gives credence to things you have been feeling, and puts into words things that were just beyond your grasp.

There are many people in this world who seem larger than life. But few of them return their gifts to the world and the souls who so desperately need them. Luis Falcao is one of those few; for he teaches not of dogma, but of the spirituality of love, and the love of spirituality.
What you will find in these pages may be just the piece of the puzzle you have been looking for.

Mark Davies, Author of the Cirillian Flame

IV. Author's Notes

Ok - So I finally give up, I am writing the book. I stand up, take a stance and speak the truth that the Creator has shared with me.

So many friends and people I have counselled have urged me to put my experiences and knowledge down on paper – so here it is.

If this is the first time we meet, well then, hello to you, my new friend. Yes I mean friend, because by reading my words you get into my spirit mind – my once private thoughts become yours as you read them silently to yourself.

These words in your mind may possibly become your own thoughts and so, as you think about my words (which are not actually mine, but from the Spirit), interpret them the way it best suits you and your soul. You may become enlightened, and this enlightenment is what makes us friends as we grow closer to our Creator, helping Him grow, helping us become closer to Him than ever before.

If you are wondering about your own life purpose……
Remember this: If you are still alive you have not yet reached the goal you once set for yourself before coming to Earth.

CHAPTER 1
The First Tough Lesson: Growing up Psychic

Ring, Ring,
"Hi, Luis here,"
"Hello… . My name is so and so and I got your number from a friend."
"Hi so and so, how can I help?"
"I don't know. You tell me, you're the psychic!"

I have always been a spiritual medium and a mystic. Several years ago, through the help of my two friends the intuitive Colleen Page and hypnotherapist, Evans Brown, I began conducting regressional hypnotherapy and spiritual readings guided by the Holy Spirit. My guide, Uriall, has been with me on this Earth for as long as I can remember. He is my spiritual advisor, friend and confidante. I have no special powers, none whatsoever. My gift was bestowed on me by the Creator so that I can help my fellow man by tuning in to the spiritual world and the Spirit (Some may call it the Holy Spirit). The difference between people who "see" and those who don't is the "tuning in" of their aerial – I was born with my aerial already tuned in.

Be careful what you wish for. As a young boy I wished for the gift of wisdom, and guess what – I certainly got a wise old Guide as a full-time mentor.

I have always been like this. It really got "bad" when I was a child growing up. I could not understand that the world could not see what I did, and I struggled to tell the difference between spirit and human as I saw them in the same three-dimensional manner. My gift often got me into trouble, and I would get punished for talking about the things and people (spirits) I saw.

A key point in my life happened in 1972, when at the age of five I saw my grandfather (My mother's side of the family) in the room and announced to the family that he was sitting in the lounge chair. This freaked everyone in the room out as no one saw the man and furthermore, we lived in Mozambique and he lived in Portugal. I informed the family, all staring in shock, that my grandfather had come to say goodbye. My family, by then, were used to me talking to the walls, but talking about, and to, a member of the family who was not present for them to see, was too much for them.

There were no house phones in those days, and so a day later when the family received a telegram to say that my grandfather had passed on, my family never looked at me in the same way again.

I was banned from speaking about the other side, and was told that, I must be possessed by an evil spirit. This scared the life out of me as my imagination took over and I imagined how awful I could become if someone else took over my body. This fear remained with me for most of my childhood.

To add fuel to an already raging fire I was taken by my grandmother (father's side of the family) to the local Catholic Church, where I was placed on an altar and almost drowned in holy water.

I became more frightened of the priest and the ritual he had conducted than I ever had been of anyone else in the world. This episode in my young life was enough to stop me from telling anyone in my family what I saw. Funnily enough, my grandfather has been in my life ever since and,

A School Called Earth

although, he is not a primary guide, he does come in and out whenever I need some level-headed or creative help. To add to his sense of humour, he dresses like a priest.

My dear mom cautioned me not to speak of it at school and this made it worse as schoolyards and playgrounds are full of angels and guides. My mother understood what was happening to me as her mother, Cristina, "spoke to the dead". My mother had inherited the gift of clairexistence from her and never stifled my curiosity in a world that no one could see. Out of concern for my wellbeing, however, she constantly warned me against telling anyone. Mozambique turned into a civil war nightmare, and my parents escaped to South Africa with only their lives.

As a young child and as a refugee in South Africa, the situation worsened. At school I was the subject of severe racial discrimination and this led me to become introverted. Strangely, as I became more of a loner, my gift began to grow. The other side were the only friends I could talk to and they never looked upon me with hatred and condescension. Uriall, who is ever comical at the best of times, took on the form of the comic hero Batman, and convinced me that one day I, too, could become a super hero. He convinced me that one day people would accept me and that one day they would even love me.

There were other loners in the school, just like me. These were children who often got bullied by other, bigger children and victimised by the teachers because they kept themselves to themselves. These children were the poorer ones from the other side of the tracks (there really was a railway line that divided the poorer suburbs from the rich ones), and they generally looked scruffier as their parents did not have the money to buy them new uniforms every year. These children, like me, lived off donations and second-hand clothes. Getting fed was our priority, and so

A School Called Earth

clothes meant little to us. We did not realise that we looked poorer, but it must have shown.

Some of the teachers themselves were racist towards any person of colour and my dark, olive skin was perfect for them to vent their insecurities about the future of the changing South Africa. This adult behaviour made the situation worse because young children mimic adults and so the teasing, discrimination, ostracisation and bullying continued.

Anyone that knows me knows that I am not one to surrender to bullies and so I fought back. One day, in my grade one year, while waiting for the school bus, I got beaten up so badly by a group of standard ten boys, that they left me for dead. They did not want a "kaffir-boetie" catching a whites-only bus, and so I was taught "a lesson". They left me in a pool of blood on the side of the road. I was missing for two days as I lay unconscious, but I had help.

When my mother, with the aid of a friendly black policeman (Ben) found me in the bushes next to the bus stop, they saw two figures standing over me when they found me. According to Ben and my mother, these two people just vanished into thin air. Being hospitalised with broken ribs, a cracked skull and almost loosing my eye, did not stop me from getting a hiding from my father for being weak.

I started to hate humans, especially adults, and this made me withdraw from society even more. The lonelier I felt, the more it compounded my hatred. Luckily for me a dear friend of the family and local karate instructor (Sensei Lappies Laubuschagne) saw my potential spiral downwards into a dangerous, rebellious path and offered to teach me the Okinawan art of karate in return for washing his car and mowing the lawn. Karate became my salvation and, like the comic book hero, I put

A School Called Earth

on an imaginary costume, fuelled by the desire to protect myself from the humiliation of getting beaten up. I did not want to be constantly scared of older children and teachers who took their fragile insecurities out on innocent young children like myself anymore.

I took on bullies as a mission in life (a cause which I still take on today) and soon I became a vicious and feared child. I would scout the world for bullies, and woe the kid who hurt another. Soon most of the school (including kids much older than I) feared me, and I loved the role. I was clearly on a path spiralling towards hatred and destruction.

To compound matters, things on the home front were not much better. My father, a policeman, was a violent and abusive alcoholic. He had spent many years in war situations and he brought them home with him. He, like many other Portuguese people in South Africa at the time, had lost everything in the civil war and in South Africa probably experienced racism himself. However, instead of lashing out at the people and colleagues that sent it his way, the bully took it out on his family – the very people who loved and adored him.

My mother was the subject of continuous verbal abuse, which turned to physical violence when alcohol was added. Pretty soon I got involved and so too I became a punch bag – one that punched back. I cannot recall how many times he broke my nose, or how many times I was hospitalised with fractured ribs and bones. All I can remember is that fighting back made me a whole lot stronger and braver. I am the eldest son of four children and I made it my duty to protect my sisters and brother. They were too young to experience any of the physical violence, but lived in dreaded fear of the fighting and verbal rage my father brought home every night. Faking sleep became the only way we coped as children, and our imaginations would soon have us escaping the terrible reality

A School Called Earth

of our childhood life. My friends from the other side used everything in their power to help us escape and we often compared the same escapist dreams the next morning.

Whenever the situation got really bad I would pray to Uriall and Gabriel (She would visit me from time to time to) and their love would give me the courage to get up in the morning and face the fear of going to school. This was my favourite prayer and I pray it to this day.

Angel of mine, my friend endears.
To whom God's love commits me here
Ever this day and night be at my side
To light and Guide
To rule and guard
Amen.

By the time I turned 16 (I had reached my black belt) there was not a child or bully I knew that dared to challenge me or hurt any person I cared for. Like everything in life, there was some good to this. As protector of the weaker bullied kids, I became their friend. As you will learn, it's the really advanced souls that take on the harsh lessons early on in life. And so I became surrounded by a really "unusual" group of friends that today are far greater achievers than those popular kids at school will ever be.

As I grew up, I spoke less and less of the other side, putting the visions and visits down to my overactive and creative imagination. Anyway, they never really helped, or so I thought.

Even as a hormonal teenager, fixated on girls and parties, I could not escape the memory of what had happened to me several years before. One morning at the age of nine, I woke to a bright light in my room. In

A School Called Earth

the middle of the bright light in my room stood what appeared to be a man with blond hair and a bright white garment. He addressed me as Michael and asked what I wanted. I was not afraid of this man, as I had seen spirits before. I recognised him as one of my family members from the other side. I asked for wisdom so that I could understand why people disliked me. I wanted to understand how I could help them. I wanted to know what I needed to do to be able to teach them to love. He asked me if I was sure about this request. When I confirmed my request He smiled and disappeared. I told no one of this visit.

Later on in life as a university student, I took on bold and ambitious challenges and ended up on the student council fighting for humanitarian causes. Drawing posters of "Free Mandela" made me realise that there were others that had experienced lessons far harsher than I ever had and so, as in all things of the spiritual awakening, the loop was made. I no longer blamed the angels and guides for not helping me, and realised that there must be a reason why they could or would not.

To pay for my studies and support my family (I had moved my mother, two sisters and brother out of my father's house) I started working as a bodyguard. This often dangerous and demanding work calls for precise planning and intuition if you are to keep your principal safe. Guess what? I started connecting with the other side in order to ensure safety for my clients and myself.

Bodyguarding instilled in me a sense of purpose and made me feel needed as I yet again protected people with a fear of others. It was a good exercise for my senses but, because there was very little exchange of positive energy and far too many negative beings around, it soon exhausted my spirit and my physical body. Furthermore, the bodyguard world was full of gung-ho individuals who lived on the need to kill, strange

A School Called Earth

as it may seem for a profession that seems hell-bent on saving lives.

Even as a bodyguard I pursued my studies in architecture and, once I was qualified, I left the body-guarding world to practise my educational learnings.

I moved on into the highly demanding world of corporate business. Again I shut out the spirit world and drew knowledge from it only when I needed strategic direction. I made good money, married a beautiful person and bought all the "right" toys. Even though I was admired by my colleagues and clients and was considered to be really good at what I did, I was still completely frustrated with life.

Fortunately for me there is, as you all know, no stopping the Creator and the destined cosmic karma (planning from the other side in which we as souls partake). I began getting severe headaches, which turned to migraines and they kept getting worse. This was all made worse as the company I was working for was going through restructuring and, as the youngest senior executive, my job was seriously on the line. Fear of loosing the house, the Harley and the fancy toys made the migraines appear more severe and finally, thank God, I was diagnosed with a cystic brain tumour.

Yes, strange as it may sound, I do mean thank God. You see the tumour was my wake-up call. This realisation made me do a "Jerry McGuire", take my goldfish and start all over again.

Chemotherapy was not for me and through a friend I was lead to Biocom resonance healing. The tumour vanished in about 3 months and in its place came my spiritual and psychic rebirth. Since then I have gone on to build a successful one-man consulting business and I truly love what I do.

A School Called Earth

In my everyday job, I help people who work for large companies. I do not really care about their corporate firms I care for the individuals who work there: their souls, their peace and their future. I used my gift to help them become successful and find the ultimate truth. After all we all have the truth inside us. As humans we search the whole world to find ourselves, but if we only searched inside ourselves we would find the whole universe.

So now that I have found security and inner peace I can see, hear and sense more clearly. I have come to the realisation that I cannot keep quiet anymore. I have to speak of the other side, of the truths I know and see and I have to help people find their way and give them affirmation that the other side exists. Teaching people about our real home and the fascinating place we go to when our bodies die, gives them hope, and connecting with their passed loved ones gives them the proof that the other side really exists. I know that in the not too distant future, this is all I will do, but for now I am happy with balancing the two worlds in one life.

We teach best that which we most seek to learn

Meet Uriall
In the past few years my spirit guide has become really loud and challenging. Through his guidance and that of the Holy Spirit, I have been lead to wonderful books by authors such as Richard Bach, Michael Newton and Silvia Browne. Reading their wisdom, I realised that I had to speak up – especially living here on the southernmost tip of Africa – a continent where so many advanced souls have come to grow their spiritual wisdom in this really tough school I call Earth.
And so I would like to introduce you to my spirit guide Uriall. The first time I met Uriall on Earth, was around 1410 AD (back home we are part of the same soul group, and thus have known each other forever). In 1410

we were both warriors in the Scottish highlands and even there he was already taking the role of my mentor. We were best friends, on a path to do-good and fight for justice together. We enjoyed a good battle (sounds absurd) especially if it meant getting rid of a tyrant and way back then he vowed to watch over me in future lives "should he go home early". I had no idea of what he meant then, but I am really glad he stuck to his promise.

Uriall – you sing it more than you say it (You – ri - aaall) - has always been with me. He still sometimes presents himself in his highlander coat of armour, but generally he prefers to look like a priest. He has guided me through several lives and is the wisest most intriguing being I have ever met. He also has the weirdest sense of humour, and is the only living person (okay spirit) I know that dares to laugh at my foolishness.

Uriall communicates with me in several ways, and he is the reason that my readings with clients are so accurate. Even the critics are amazed! I can hear his voice, he sends me mental pictures like a plasma TV screen, gives me smells and odours, sounds and even sends me tastes.

I still cannot explain exactly how it works or why the Creator has chosen me as a channel (I prefer to be called a messenger). All I know is that it is fairly accurate and it gives many people hope and courage.

Although I been psychic my whole life, it was only after reading books on the subject of psychic phenomena that I came familiar with the terminology used to describe these talents. I have the gift of clairvoyance, clairexistence and clairaudience: sometimes only one gift a time, sometimes a combination of two gifts and sometimes all three together, depending on the level of spirit trying to contact me. Mostly I am what you would call claircognisant. I just get a sense of knowing, as if I am the person I am reading or trying to help.

A School Called Earth

A psychic person (The real ones at least) has the ability to predict your future and or past. I feel that they do this by tapping into your energy and since your future, past and present is all in the make-up of your soul's energy they can get a glimpse of your life and tell you the future. Please always be very careful when consulting a psychic. They may very well be seeing your future, but you have something called free will and choice, and with all good intentions, the psychic may lead you to the wrong conclusion that would then be lead you to the wrong choice.

I have the same ability as any predictive psychic, but I am not interested in these tap-ins into fortune-telling. I have been graciously given a gift that enables me to talk to souls, angels and guides on the other side and all around us and, as you can imagine, this is a lot more rewarding and inspiring than being a fortune cookie. My work is for the Creator and His Creation, not for the entertainment of mankind.

How using psychics can lead you to make the wrong choice and eventually move you far away from your right path.

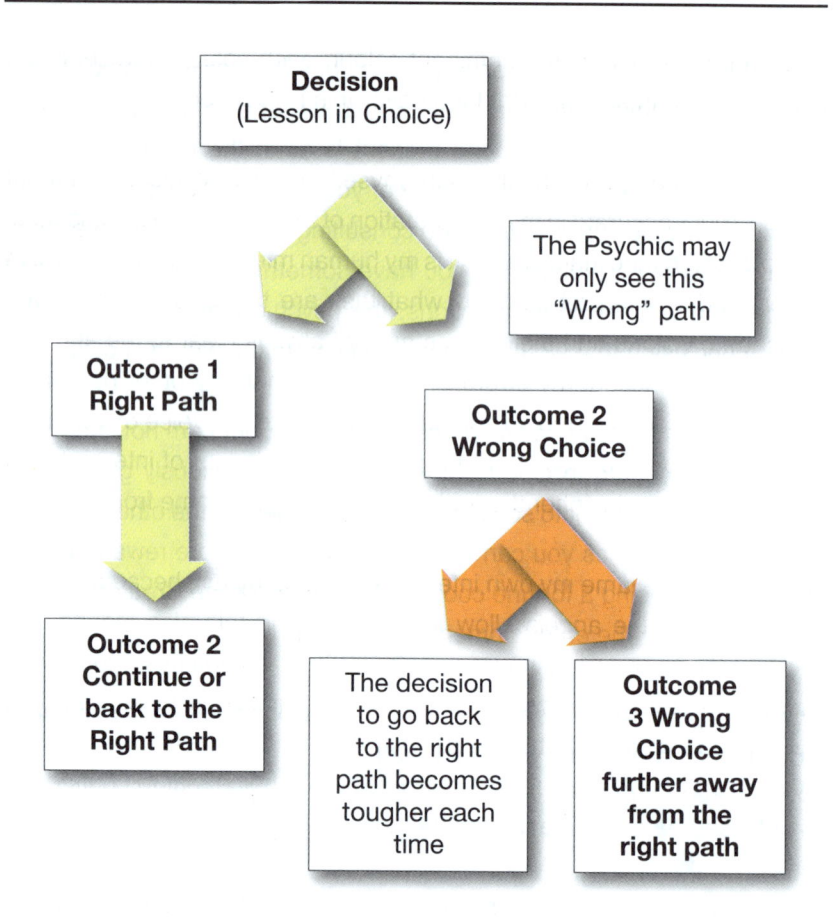

```
                    ┌─────────────────────┐
                    │      Decision       │
                    │  (Lesson in Choice) │
                    └─────────────────────┘
                             │
                  ┌──────────┴──────────┐
                  ▼                     ▼
                                ┌──────────────────┐
                                │  The Psychic may │
                                │   only see this  │
                                │   "Wrong" path   │
                                └──────────────────┘
    ┌──────────────┐
    │  Outcome 1   │
    │  Right Path  │            ┌──────────────┐
    └──────────────┘            │  Outcome 2   │
           │                    │ Wrong Choice │
           │                    └──────────────┘
           ▼                           ▲
                              ┌────────┴────────┐
    ┌──────────────┐    ┌─────────────┐   ┌──────────────┐
    │  Outcome 2   │    │The decision │   │   Outcome    │
    │ Continue or  │    │  to go back │   │  3 Wrong     │
    │  back to the │    │ to the right│   │   Choice     │
    │  Right Path  │    │path becomes │   │further away  │
    └──────────────┘    │tougher each │   │  from the    │
                        │    time     │   │  right path  │
                        └─────────────┘   └──────────────┘
```

Meet my critic

I am by nature a very critical person, and this means that I am my own worst critic. People often ask me for proof of my talents. If they only knew that I am *always* asking for it myself.

I can and always have seen the souls of people who once lived on this earth and who, one day, will be back again. I have always seen the various colours of these magnificent beings inside all humans, and through my regression research sessions into the afterlife, I now understand their

A School Called Earth

meaning. Each soul has a dominant colour, each colour representing a different stage in soul growth. I will cover this facet later.

Some days, however, I really doubt myself and my abilities. I am not always 100% accurate in the interpretation of the spirit world's messages. It's not that they are inaccurate – it is my human mind that does not always understand or interpret correctly what they are trying to communicate. Messages, visions and their voices are not always clear to me and so I have come to accept my errors. I also doubt that any other psychic is ever 100% accurate, and so should you. Listen to the voice of your own guide and allow the Holy Spirit to give you the wisdom of interpretation and the ability to decipher the truth, wherever it may come from.

For the errors I blame my own interpretation and myself, because I know that Uriall and the angels allow for free will and this also means free interpretation. They are never wrong, it's that sometimes I just don't interpret the messages properly. But when I think back to all the hope, courage and wisdom that Uriall, the guides and the angels have given to my clients through me, I realise that I have no choice, but to continue in this blessed path the Creator has bestowed upon me.

For the courage and the wisdom, the messages of hope and enlightenment, I give the glory to the Creator, for He alone knows all. To those of you who think my own life lessons are harsh, please do not compare them to your life. My toughest moments are as tough to me as the toughest you have ever had. There are millions out there who have had it a lot worse than I. I do not think it makes my lessons any less severe – especially at the time they are happening. Our realities are different – accept and embrace your reality and remember no one has a perfect view of the world, and who's to say any specific view is right?

I thank my Creator for giving me the opportunity to have experienced every tough lesson, and I pray that they have given me the right truth and wisdom to turn each lesson into a case study whereby I can now give back guidance and understanding to the world's souls.

Remember – do not blame the Creator for your tough lessons, but thank Him that He has had the faith in you to allow you to plan them into your life – thank Him as He stands by you and protects you as you learn and experience the lessons YOU have chosen to learn.

CHAPTER 2
The Creator

God, the Creator

I prefer to call God the Creator. I believe, because I have sensed His presence more than I have seen Him, that the Creator is greater than One. For the sake of simplicity I have used the pronoun "He" to denote God, but by He I mean all that is God. I believe that there is firstly the Creator or Father God, secondly there is the Mother God or the Holy Spirit of God and thirdly the Son of God or the Creation of the highest evolved Souls, the Christed Soul, of which the best known would be Jesus Christ, Buddha etc. The Creator made us all. In creating us He gave us His energy in the form of our souls. We, therefore, are a part of the Creator. In all of us lives God. We are, therefore, God even though few of us accept or understand the God in all of us. Because of our hierarchical society, we rather choose to rank the Creation and place God at the top, thus passing all responsibility to Him.

I am not religious. I do not follow any specific religion to worship my Creator. I am one who lives in the spirit of my Creator. I constantly talk to the Creator and I constantly get messages back. Sometimes the messages are direct and sometimes they come via a guide, an angel and sometimes through a fellow human.

I do not believe there is only one path to enlightenment. There are many paths to the TRUTH. I believe everyone should follow the one path that works for him. You all have a conscience, and you all know inherently when something is right or wrong. We are all given the ability to feel good or to feel shame. We know when we are helping others and when we are harming others. We often just choose to ignore our inner voices and inner feelings, and choose a religion that suits our "feel-good-factor" inside. We all have free will and our only obligation to the Creator is to be true to ourselves. Follow your own truth and your own path. To be true to a path or person that does not resonate with your soul is to be untrue to the Creator, and it is not only impossible to sustain but also the mark of a false life.

I do not condone or condemn any religion, nor do I think anyone should. I find it unthinkable that young impressionable souls in earthly bodies are given to harming each other in the name of a spiritual path to the Creator's truth. Never has the Creator asked His people to harm one another - people have, and often use, religion and the religion's devout followers to carry out their self-centred ambitions. Little do they know that if you kill or harm another being using the Creator's Truth as a weapon – His paths to enlightenment as a way to fulfil their power-hungry desires, that the harshness that they sow, they shall eventually reap.

I believe that you should follow whatever path gives you inner peace and hope for the afterlife. Go with your gut feel. This is how your soul knows it will reach its intended journey to living its intended lessons. Live for the Creator and do whatever makes you live in harmony with your fellow man. Remember all of the Creator's people have souls, so if you harm, judge or criticise another you are harming, judging or criticising the Creator's creations. Who the hell do you think you are and furthermore, what gives you the right to criticise?

The Holy Trinity
The Catholic religion speaks of the Holy Trinity. I wonder if they know how close to the truth they really are. The Catholic faith defines the Holy Trinity as God the Father, God the Son (Jesus) and God the Holy Spirit. In my soul memory (And that of my regression clients) what I see is

A School Called Earth

very similar. There is the Father Creator (Male Dominant energy), the Creator Mother (Female Dominant energy) and the Son Creator (The Creators energy in all Souls) The Father and Mother Creator together form what we call God, Creators of all Creation (and I will refer to all of the Creators as Creator for the sake of simplicity). Their energy is pure love and is made up of sound and light. Their Creation family consists of the angels and all the souls in the entire universe. Many of these souls have incarnated on this planet and so the Creator has sent some very special and highly advanced souls, that are as close to the Creator as a soul can get, down to this planet to help the rest of us souls progress through soul evolvement.

These highly evolved special souls are the enlightened ones, who we often call God or the Sons of God, but they are very much like the rest of us souls. The only difference between us, and these enlightened souls that we have called God, is that they have reached enlightenment. These enlightened souls (Christians call him Jesus, Buddhists call him Buddha etc) have brought us spiritual paths to enlightenment, but unfortunately these various different paths have become the religions of this world, that now divide the human race. They never wanted us to pray to them and call them God. Human nature has done so all on its own because of our need to rank and, therefore, absolve ourselves from taking responsibility for our errors and sins. Furthermore, we have chosen to follow only one path and criticise the others, forgetting that they are all paths in which we can reach the same destination called enlightenment; paths back to a oneness with our Creator.

Because of the diversity of this planet, the various enlightened "Sons of God" came down in different areas of the world and taught the same path to the same Creator in different ways and times, so that the people they were teaching could understand the lessons in a manner that was

A School Called Earth

relevant to their lives. These highly evolved souls are what I like to call the enlightened souls. They are one with the Creator's light and energy. They are the true Sons of God in every respect.

Why different religions then? Why did the Creator not ensure that we all have the same path to enlightenment – eternal life etc? Well, because there is free will. We as souls are continuously evolving and therefore our lessons need several perspectives for us to understand all angles of the wisdom.

As we grow closer to the Creator we learn different lessons. This makes us all wiser and more knowledgeable. There are so many things to learn about, so many histories, theories and lessons. Do you really think that you are going to learn everything in one life, at one stage on this Earth and only in one culture with only one religion with only one perspective with only one body type with only one sex – get the message?

Understand this, even if it's the only thing you get from reading this book: why would the Creator create a little baby and then let the baby die at birth? What could that soul possibly learn? How demented do you think the Creator is that He would create a life just to see it extinguish in its first few days on Earth? Why would The Creator create a baby, let it be born into this world and then ask it to come back just so that the Creator could have this baby's soul back in heaven to love? Why would the Creator not just create a soul up in heaven and then keep that soul in heaven? Do you think the Creator has created a baby soul as entertainment for Himself? How selfish do you think the Creator is? – WAKE UP! The Creator is about unconditional love and He loves us more than we could ever imagine. Every life, every hardship, every challenge is a gift that teaches us an invaluable lesson that ultimately leads us to enlightenment; to a stage I call Being in Oneness with the Creator.

A School Called Earth

Those of you who are parents know that eventually that little baby will become a growing child with a need for knowledge and that one day you would have to let it go to school, one day have to let it go to university, and one day have to let it become whatever it chooses to be.

You all know that children who grow up to become whatever the parents wanted them to be are usually miserably unhappy and will only find peace when they eventually go out and do whatever they wanted to.

As parents you get the most joy out of your children when they grow and flourish, become successful in whatever they choose and find happiness their own way and eventually thank you because you did the one most important thing – the only real thing that counts – you loved them unconditionally for who they really are and for who they want to be. You did not have children so they can keep you company for the rest of your life, because you love them.

Life is about learning from the consequences of the choices we make. Stopping the choice being made just delays the lesson. Consider the following scenario (those of you who have small children are highly aware of this constant challenging thought). If you only had one choice from the following two options to make for your children, which one would you choose? One, would you prefer them to grow up and become rich and successful or, two, would you prefer them to grow up and find joy and love but not be very wealthy? Pick one because it is eventually their choice and since you are not the Creator you cannot plan every aspect of their lives, hence you could not pick a third choice (which some of you wanted to do) which was for your children to be rich and successful and find joy and love. Ultimately, you as a parent can try and make the best choices for you children but one day, when you are no longer around, regardless of what the best laid plans you have left behind are, they will have to fend for themselves and make their own choices. Eventually the lessons you so lovingly thought you protected them from, will have to be learned.

Continuous growth

The Creator is not static. The Creator is ever growing, and as we grow and become more knowledgeable, enlightened and wise, the Creator grows. As our love for one another grows so the Creator becomes more fulfilled and satisfied with the work that he has created. Like a brilliant artist, even though he may be really good at painting, he will continue to paint. Even though the spectators of the art may think that the artwork is brilliant and that the artist has reached perfection, the artist himself knows there is room for improvement, even if it means painting something that he has never painted before. Painting for the artist is what he does because he loves it and it fulfils him. Creating for the Creator is what he does because He loves it and it fulfils Him too.

We are all brothers and sisters, interconnected as souls, part of the Creator and a part of His continuous growth. He wants us to learn everything He knows. You do not learn by listening alone, you do it by experiencing and by teaching. So, too, we get to learn the Creator's lessons by listening to the Creator's teachings through our spirit guides, the angels and each other. Most of all we get to learn by living our lives, experiencing the diversity of its lessons and eventually by guiding and teaching others.

There are so many advanced and good souls on this earth that help other souls in their own way. Some are religious teachers, some educational teachers and some teach by the lives they live. If only those teachers realised that, in essence, we all pretty much teach the same lessons, albeit in different ways with slightly different analogies. We must learn to accept that we are all different for a reason, and that reason is because

A School Called Earth

our Creator chose to learn many lessons in different ways Himself. Learn to accept others for what they are and for how they chose to be on this earth. Don't condemn differences but rather embrace them because you might still have to experience it for yourself one day.

Just in case you feel alone, the Creator sends us angels and guides to help us with growing and learning. We have guides on earth and back at home. I will cover them in following chapters.

Learning lessons on this Earth plane is putting to practise what your Soul already has learnt on the other side in theory. You will practise the lesson until you get it right

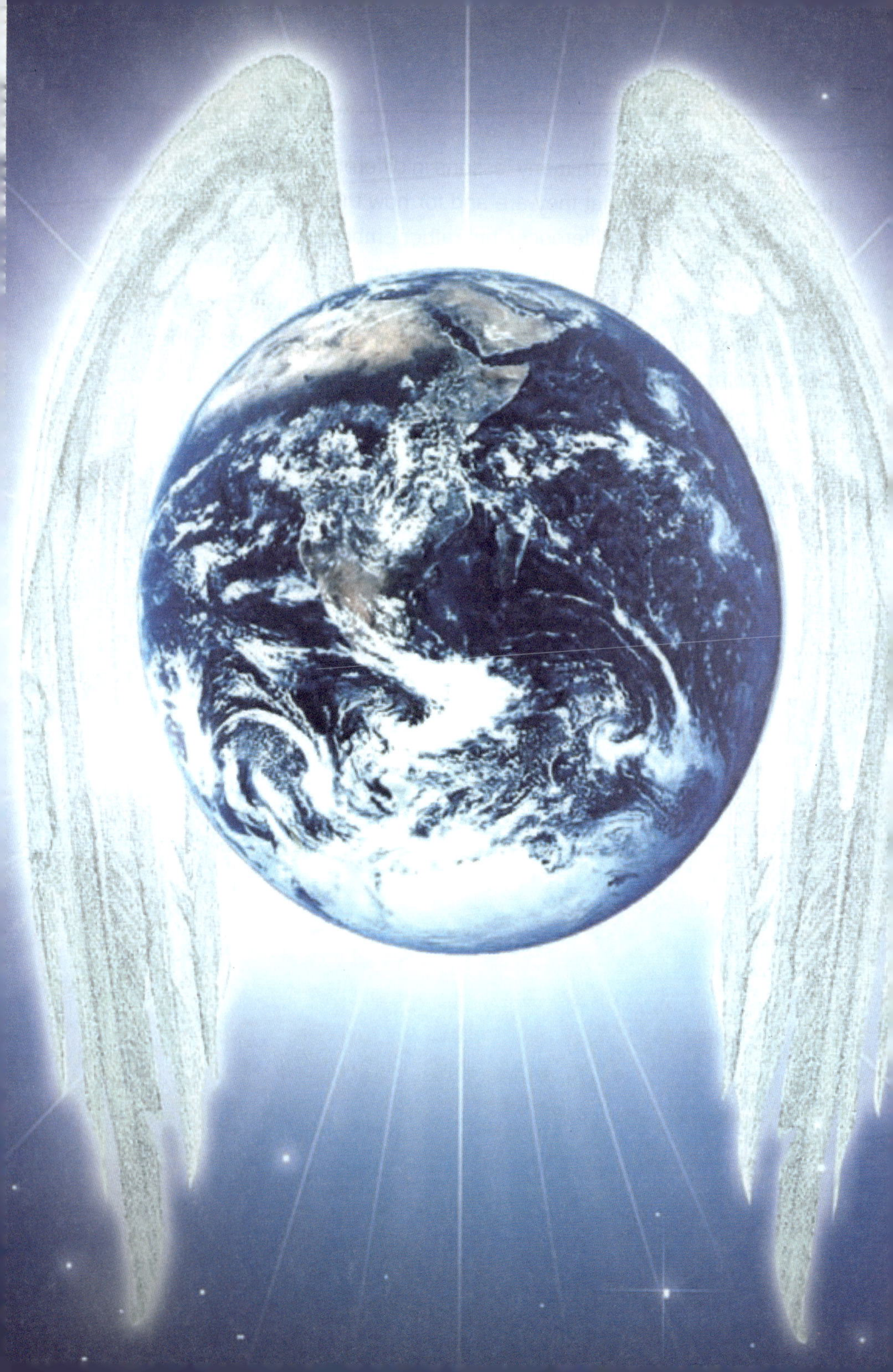

CHAPTER 3
How It All Works - Life On The Other Side

What are you?
You are not your body. You are an everlasting soul within a spiritual being that occupies a body on this planet. Your soul is part of the Creator. You are the expansion of the Creator, given to growth through the gaining of knowledge and wisdom, which is gained through experience on planets like the earth and others. Your spirit is the vessel that the Creator has given you for your soul to learn and grow. The challenge for your spirit is to lose the need for personal identity and become one with the soul. In the spirit world, souls that have not yet reached enlightenment retain their spirit form, as the soul provides the spirit with the energy that gives it shape. As this merger between soul and spirit evolves, the spirit will cease to exist and the soul will go back to oneness with the Creator. For the purpose of simplicity I will call both spirit and the soul energy within a human, a soul.

Your body is a vessel chosen by your spirit to get by on this planet. Think of it as a company car. Take care of it as if it is your own car even though it may not be the type of car you would have bought should you have paid with your own money.

We will talk about your body later. If you think for one second of what will happen to you when you die, even the biggest non-believer must surely feel that something of yourself will be left behind. That which you feel is left behind is your spirit. The mind and driving energy of the spirit is your soul. This soul is a part of the Creator, and thus a part of the Creator is in all of us. We all have God, The Creator in us and therefore we all are a part of God. In truth we are God.

A School Called Earth

Your body would not, and could not, function properly without a spirit with soul energy. Your soul gives energy to your spirit. Your spirit is what drives your body – think of it like that company car with the driver being the spirit and the brain and energy of the driver being the soul. (For the purpose of simplicity and to avoid confusion, I will continue to talk of the spirit with soul within as soul).

Your brain is a super engine. But without purpose, without intent and a road map, this engine has no use. You can start the engine and it will run on its own for a while, but without a driver the car will go nowhere. And so, like a company car with an engine, driven by a driver with a purpose of getting to a certain destination, your soul (the driver) has a vessel with a brain that helps you get to a pre-determined destination set out by a map brought to this life with you.

Don't get me wrong, we all have free will, but this will has been decided by you long before you are born. You still have choices along the way, but you and your caretakers on the other side have carefully planned even the outcome of those choices. A body without a soul would be like a primitive human, focusing only on selfish needs, as it would have no conscience whatsoever.

What does the soul within the spirit look like?
For the record - I do not see auras. Auras are the colours given off by the body due to its energy field. I also do not see chakras or energy points. The body's auras and chakras have various colours but are not the colour of your soul. I see the souls inside each human. Each soul is completely unique and each one is different in colour. Up until I read Michael Newton's book – *The Journey Of Souls* (Llewellyn Publications, 2002) I was not completely certain what was meant. Souls are within the spirit and are shaped much like a cigar. This cigar shape is a little

A School Called Earth

swollen around the top. In the centre of this soul is a dominant colour. The colours change towards the outside, ending with a bright white.

These layers of colour are the stages and lessons learnt by the soul. Every time the soul advances it gets more colours to the centre and so the external colours show the earlier stages of the Soul. It's much like the rings of a tree, except in reverse. The layers of colour show the experiences of the soul, with the outer layers are the first colours.

Figure 1: A Soul inside a body

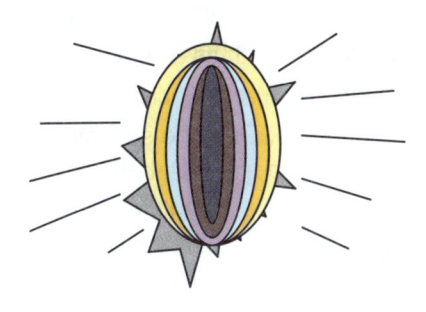

Souls are differentiated from each other via colours and shape. In the spirit world we often take on a particular shape of a life we enjoyed on earth. Most of the differentiation happens via vibrational communication, though. Souls communicate via a telepathic language and souls of a certain soul group resonate to a similar frequency. We have no problem finding each other, it happens as soon as you think of the other soul.

Souls have no facial features. The head area looks very much like a cloudy oval with two darker patches where the eyes ought to be. I have never seen a mouth, and I have never heard them speak. When they communicate, it's pretty much via thoughts. When I am doing a reading and a past loved one's soul comes through, they will appear to me in the shape/body of their past life. They do this so that I can identify them and relate them to my client. Souls project or transmit a picture or scene to me so that my client may get a confirmation of the soul that has come through.

They generally keep the shape for the duration of their visit and then whisk away once it is time for them to depart.

Souls are the kindest, most sincere and most caring form of "human" I have ever met (I only call them "human" because I distinguish between human souls and angel-like beings). They have no anger, fear, hate or any of the human characteristics that make us weak or hurtful to each other. By the time you come to earth as a soul (in a psychic reading or as a guide to your earthbound soul) or reincarnate as a person, your soul is back to its most perfect state. Only the schoolground taints a soul as it grows and learns.

Figure 2: A spirit in its pure form

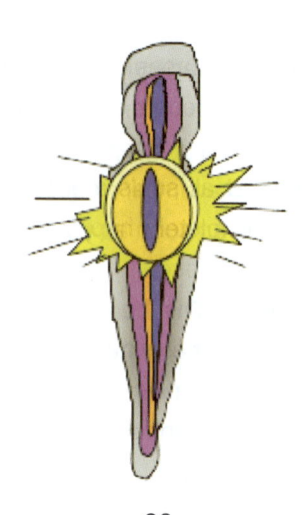

A School Called Earth

How is a soul born?

In my understanding and interpretation of my regression research, I believe that new souls are being born continually. If what I have seen on the other side is, however, not in any way connected to a linear time frame whatsoever, then I admit I may be mistaken because the young baby souls I saw being born may have been born in the past with no relation to earth time and, therefore, they were born before the earth was created – meaning that there is a possibility (albeit slight due to my spiritual sense which is 80% accurate) that they have all been born and no more new ones are created. However our Creator is infinite and so is His growth, hence the logical explanation is that His creation is infinite and, therefore, forever growing.

In my understanding and interpretation of what I have seen in my spiritual visions, there is no finite number of souls because the Creator is infinite. I know it's difficult to imagine, but this is one of those times where I am going to ask you to take my word for it. Souls are created in a special maternity sphere, where they are nurtured and taken care of by a special group of mother souls. These souls love this task so much that when they incarnate on this earth, I find them in a similar position. These souls on earth take on tasks such as nurses or primary school teachers where they can take care of the small people and help them along.

I would also like to state that all souls are completely at peace in the spirit world, as they are completely happy just "being". Being in this world is when you are in the present, with no thoughts, no stress and no fear. Most of us experience this "being" state sometime in our lives, but, unfortunately, as soon as we allow our minds to replace "being", with thoughts of the past or future, we lose the peaceful euphoria of the soul.

Imagine the Creation

Your imagination is bound by your wisdom and creativity. Even so it is beautiful.

Now think of what our Creator has imagined with His infinite wisdom.

What happens when we die?
This is not meant to offend any religion or to contradict any belief. As I have said before, please take in whatever resonates with you, and the rest you can ignore. This is what I have seen in my many past lives and in the death situations I can remember. More importantly, though, my regression research has validated my memories of the spirit world.

For those of you who fear death, I hope this brings you some hope and takes away some of your fear. The soul is a part of the Creator and is, therefore, eternal. It will continue reincarnating for as long as it feels it needs to learn lessons provided by the earth school.

When the soul leaves the body it usually moves home (some call it Heaven, the Other Side, you can call it whatever makes you happy). This journey home is slightly different for some, as each soul prefers a different tempo and a different atmosphere for departure from this world.

You are limited by the boundaries of what you can perceive

A School Called Earth

I am going to describe the commonalities that my clients have described under regression therapy and what I can remember from my past journeys home. When the body stops working and the mind switches off in its final breath, the soul exits the body.

The length of time that a soul lingers around the body varies from soul to soul. My understanding is that the younger souls who have not incarnated many times tend to stay and watch what happens to the departing. Some even want to see who comes to the funeral so as to check on who really cares about them. Some stick around to say goodbye to their loved ones. Some stay for a long time.

As the soul leaves the body it gets a gentle magnetic pull. This pull takes you through a cloudy mass shaped like a spiralling tunnel. There is often a light at the end of this tunnel but the walls of the tunnel are see-through and I get the feeling that the soul travels through a Milky Way type of environment. Somewhere during the journey, the soul will become aware of humming and voice-like sounds.

As the soul travels further down the tunnel, the atmosphere becomes a light plasma-like environment. At this time the soul is greeted by loving souls such as their guides or loved ones who have passed. Angels are always nearby to guide and protect us. Often our angels will appear to the soul (who still has the earth memories) like our religious messiah (such as Jesus or Buddha), to give us the peace we would associate with going to Heaven.

The journey often takes us past the soul's home which looks to me like an endless string of large spheres, all interconnected and all flowing into a central core of energy. If you look at it from a distance it looks like a huge group of DNA strings all spiralling into a black hole (except it's all

A School Called Earth

colourful and ends in bright light). These huge spheres are where souls live in large groups of up to 1000 souls. We will cover these spheres later.

The soul then arrives in a large room-like sphere where its guides, loved ones and a group of caretakers welcome it home. The soul then undergoes a shower of cleansing where we get rid of the past life's damage and negative energy. None of the past lessons get lost in the soul's memory, just the pain, hurt, humiliation and fear get washed away.

The soul emerges from this shower cleansed and pure and re-energised with the Creator's love. The soul will have all its past lives memories and will be completely familiar with its guides, angels and watchers (See Soul Roles). The soul is then taken to the "Hall of Knowledge" where it gets to examine its past lives. The place where I go looks much like a Roman Temple, except that the walls are always shifting. I always get the feeling of being loved and handled with kid gloves. In this hall we are greeted by a group of Wise Elders. These Elders are a group of advanced souls who have stopped incarnating and are there to help us learn from our past lives.

They have pretty much "been there done that" and so, because of their experience and the fact that they are filled with the loving kindness of the Creator, they are not judgemental. I do get the feeling that they feel disappointment if we have not achieved what we had set out to learn, but there is no "bad boy" attitude. We get to look at our past life and the choices we made. They comment on how we could have acted in some situations and congratulate us on our successes. As I have said before, this council is magnificent and the elders are the kindest form of love; the only earthly feeling that comes close to this is being in the company of Angels while on earth. Being in their presence is truly to be

A School Called Earth

anointed and an awe-inspiring experience. One I will never forget. Once this experience is complete we get to go home – to our destination as souls.

As the soul arrives at its final destination it is greeted by loved ones. Many souls that we have known in our lives that have passed on come and greet us, as well as souls from our previous lives that we may not have met in our most recent life. There is usually much hugging (a type of merging) and love shared in these situations. This is as close as it gets to a child's birthday party. Well, it is a kind of a birth date, I guess.

Souls live in large clusters. As I have mentioned before these clusters consisting of up to one thousand souls, are housed in large spheres that are all interconnected. In each sphere there are smaller group spheres consisting of up to fifty souls. These souls belong to classroom-type clusters. These are your secondary family of souls. These souls are all of a similar soul-age group and they attend classroom-type educational groups. In this group of fifty souls, there are small groups of souls known as soul families. These small family soul groups range from between five to ten souls.

When a soul is born, Nurturer Souls take care of and guide it until it is ready to go to school. This "school" consists of many soul classrooms consisting of approximately fifty souls per class. There are many classrooms in a school, which in turn make up a school of approximately one thousand souls. Each classroom has a teacher. This teacher also attends a school classroom himself/herself, but by now there will be fewer souls in the group because his/her previous classmates have either advanced to the next level or are levels behind. In soul school you graduate at your own pace until you reach the final level. Thereafter you move on to the next level where you take on a higher role such as Librarian, Planner,

A School Called Earth

Watcher, Birth Assistant, Death Receiver or Elder. These roles will be explained later.

Soul families and group structures

Soul families generally reincarnate together on earth and other planets but not all the time, as certain family members progress to higher classroom levels during their soul lives. As your soul advances so it moves up the ladder to a more advanced classroom. Some of your initial soul group members will advance with you, whereas others will stay behind. As you learn and study lessons back home you will get the opportunity to go on a field trip to school on earth! A group of you will go together, much like a field trip. This is why we find soul groups from home in and around each other on earth. On earth you will find members of your soul group occupying roles such as spouses, brothers, sisters, aunts, friends or even children. Sometimes, they are even enemies.

Life on this planet is extremely well planned by the Planner Souls and us. Every day and every experience is planned in the most amazing detail. As humans we like to blame everyone else except ourselves for what life dishes out when, in fact, we planned every aspect of our life on this earth in considerable detail. I find it amazing when humans blame God for everything. On the one hand we all acknowledge that the Creator is all-powerful and all-loving and then, on the other hand, we say that he punishes us. How or why would he punish you if the Creator is indeed all-loving and all-forgiving? Have you heard of choice? You see, the Creator is so all loving that he gives you the choice of lessons to learn and he allows you to take the harsh ones too. You have planned every aspect of your life including the loss of a loved one, a child, a spouse or a good friend. The Creator is not taking that person away from you. You, the person, and your Planner Guide planned it in every detail a long time ago. It doesn't make the experience of loss any less, but you really

A School Called Earth

should stop blaming the Creator for your plans that, you feel, have gone awry.

We plan our life paths very carefully. We choose our parents and family and we also choose our bodies. Depending on the lessons we need to learn, we will be given a variety of choices by the Planners, but the choice is finally ours. When the soul has learnt all the theory it can, back at home, it will get a sense of calling. The calling will be to put the theory to practice. When it is time to find a schoolground to put the theory to practice, your guide and master teacher will accompany you to a "future planning" dome where you will be met by the highly advanced souls I like to call the Planners. Planners no longer reincarnate, although they have in the past. They know all the lessons that souls can learn and they help us with our choices. They are careful not to steer us against our will, but they do advise against making a wrong choice.

The future-planning dome looks much like a large theatre building with many small theatres in it. You are guided to a theatre-like dome, where your planner guide shows you a series of life choices. You get to see them in detail and you get to ask as many questions as you want to. You also get to teleport yourself into the scenes where you become an observer of sorts. You get to smell all the aromas, feel the climate and hear the noises. I remember them in detail, which is why I always end up choosing lives where there is lots of good coffee!

Souls that will play a major part of your life on this earth will sporadically enter the theatre where you get to choose the roles you will play. Sometimes these roles will be quite harsh, such as in an abusive parent, but it means a lesson to both souls. The soul being the abusive parent will have to learn compassion and tolerance whereas the abused child will have to learn forgiveness and endurance. There are lessons for both souls in any given situation and this is why we should reflect on our lives no matter how hard they are and learn from them. If you don't learn, you will surely have to repeat the lesson in the next life. Once you are happy with the chosen life and body you get to say goodbye to the other side. It is not very traumatic because as far as the remaining souls are concerned you will be back soon. Time on the other side is not linear and a lifetime on Earth to us could mean a few weeks in the spirit world.

Your true family in this life is not defined by flesh and blood. Rather it is defined by your spiritual attraction to each other and the joy you share in seeing your family members attain spiritual growth.

Playgrounds and soul activity
So, besides learning in classroom-like structures, planning and guiding other souls, what do we do back home? – We play of course! Once the soul has had a "daily" education session (I say daily but this could mean chapters of learning which could take years or seconds), it can go out to the playground and play with the other souls and soul friends. Souls partake in many activities on the other side, most of which they have brought back to the earth. Here are some of the activities that some of my clients and I can remember:
- Singing in choirs
- Creating music in an orchestra or small band
- Theatre – either as actors or spectators
- Horse riding – horses exist back at home and there is a game similar to fox hunting but the fox enjoys the game because there is no harm done – just a chase for pure exhilaration. This is a

A School Called Earth

pastime I enjoy back home, and one that I sort of do on earth, except on earth the horse has an engine and the fox is the stopwatch. (I love to race motorcycles)
- Debating society type functions where strategy is key
- Games similar to soccer and rugby – although it is always fair, no referee is needed and no one ever wins. It's about the fun and not about winning
- Creation activities where souls get to invent things that get brought back to earth as ideas. We also play with energy creation and build crystal-like structures and help shape creations such as seeds and the pollination of plants
- Building – certain souls love to build things such as bridges and buildings – no guessing what they do on earth
- Dancing to music or as entertainers. This is where I met one of my soul students, Deirdre (Delfina is her Soul name). She has the most amazing grace on this earth. A quality of movement that she possesses back at home, is brought back to her lives on this earth.

As souls we love to interact with one another. We love to play which is why, as children, the playground is a source of fun to most children and adults alike. If only we kept the child and the playground within us, life would be so much more fun.

Soul roles
As Souls we all have roles to play. As young Souls most of our activities are either learning in the classroom or playing in the playground. As you learn in the classroom you get to go to practical experiments to experience the theory – you get to come to planets like earth.

A School Called Earth

As the soul matures and passes on to higher levels, it starts to take on roles with tough lessons. As the soul moves onto the old soul stage it takes on the role of teacher back at home and, as it advances through the higher levels, it gets to play the role of secondary guides to our reincarnated soul friends and soul families. As secondary guides we help the primary guides on earth, guiding our soul subject in a variety of roles. These roles vary according to our experience and the need of a reincarnated soul. For example, if one of our soul friends was a son or daughter in the past life and they pray for support from the deceased parent, we may go to them and sow comfort and love over them in order for them to get over their tough time on earth. If we are creators or inventors we may go to the assistance of a soul friend that has reincarnated as an artist and needs some spiritual creativity. Inspiration that the artist receives is a combination of his own brain ability married with his soul and the "IN-SPIRIT" guidance of the secondary soul guide.

Soul roles explained

Librarian - Advanced souls who keep the records and help us choose our next life theme.

Planner – Highly advanced souls who are master strategists and plan the interconnectivity of souls and soul lives. They safeguard karma and ensure everything flows as it should.

Watcher – Souls who watch out for us and help our guides. They are often referred to as secondary guides and can be passed loved ones (advanced souls only) who come to guide us from time to time.

Creator / Manufacturers / Builders – Souls who create energies and help heal. They often come to earth as guides of people in professions where healing the earth and animals is concerned. They also inspire us and hence the word inspiration – "In-Spirit".

A School Called Earth

Birth Assistant and Nurturer - Souls who assist the soul as it gets ready for the life on earth and the traumatic transference to the earth school.

Death Receiver. These are the souls who "meet and greet" the soul as it passes back home to the spirit world. They help with the cleansing of our earth trauma and pain. They have a healing and calming effect for the recently deceased soul, especially the younger ones.

Teacher – These old and advanced souls teach the lesser-advanced souls the various theory lessons that souls later experiment with on planets such as earth.

Master Teachers – These highly advanced souls have stopped incarnating and teach the teachers and guides at home.

Healers – These highly advanced souls help the recently crossed-over soul heal and let go of any traumatic memories they bring back from having incarnated on planets such as earth.

Elders – Extremely advanced souls who helps us analyse our past life and provide us with guidance for life path planning and analysis.

Soul Gender
Most souls prefer either the male or female gender. Souls have no sex organs but are either softer, gentler, female souls or more intense male souls. Souls generally prefer one gender projection even though they may reincarnate as the opposite sex from time to time. It explains the homosexuality on this school playing ground, as souls who prefer the female energy may battle with male bodies on earth and vice versa. Again this is free will; and we are not here to be the Creators judges. Accept people and accept souls and live peacefully and harmoniously

together. Love people, whatever they may be, because if you can love your fellow soul you are in actual fact honouring and loving the Creator's creation.

Untimely passing and helping themes
If the soul that has reincarnated on earth needs to learn the lesson of child loss, old more advanced souls can take the role of the infant that is to die young on earth. This is a lesson for the parents to learn on earth and so the advanced soul will come into the baby's body before birth, purely to assist the parent soul with the lessons. These souls leave the body quickly and move through the tunnel with lightning pace. There is still a period of cleansing, purely because birth into a human body is traumatic, to say the least.

There is no such thing as an untimely death. We plan everything in absolute detail and our destiny is written in our Hall of Records long before we incarnate. Even being murdered is planned, not that it makes the deed forgivable but, like everything in the universe, there is a reaction for every action, a benefit and a cause, a result due to an action. Everything is interconnected and, therefore, everything is a function of the whole. Accept it, it's the way the Creator planned it.

There is no such thing as coincidence other than the coincidence of the word itself

The reality is that we exit when the soul has learnt all it can, even though we as humans always believe that our lives are not complete and that there is more for us to do. Again we have planned our exit, even if we are perfectly healthy. Ever heard of the multiple gold medal tri-athlete type who dies in his sleep for no apparent reason or from a heart attack?

A School Called Earth

Because everything is interconnected, we plan our death situation in detail. Those of us that get murdered have planned the time and place and we have even met up with the murdering soul and agreed on a time and date. Of course the murdering soul has the ultimate choice of choosing not to murder (possibly a lesson that this soul needs to learn), but you will have planned a back-up exit or two – the truth is that when it's your time to go – you will.

In the case of a miracle the following happens. Your guides may intervene and ask the planners and head counsellors for an extension. Careful planning is entered into because all lives are interconnected and your extension may affect the souls on earth adversely. For example, you may have planned your exit through a terminal disease, but through prayer and healing you are saved. After your death your spouse was going to remarry a soul from her group (say a soul that also lost a spouse and desperately wants to start over) and together they were going to learn a lesson of loving again, restarting afresh, and grieving the death of passed loved ones. Now that you have been given an extension, that other soul needs to find a similar spouse on earth with whom it can learn the planned lessons, without affecting the pre-destined plan of the alternative soul. Gets complex, doesn't it? However, it explains why miracles of this sort are few and far between. But don't stop believing and having hope, because the planners are super strategists and planning is what they live for. They love a challenge and there is always free will.

Suicide – Is there Punishment?
Again this is a question that gets asked often and one in which humans have somehow managed to completely misinterpret the teachings and wisdom of past prophets and teachers.

There are the very few cases when a soul exits as part of a suicide that was planned in order to teach the remaining souls a lesson. In these cases

A School Called Earth

the soul in question plans the suicide in detail with the interconnected souls that needs to learn lessons of forgiveness and bereavement at the same time. The soul that exits via suicide would have planned to learn all its lessons before the suicide act and chooses the act as the exit point. These souls come to earth with suicide as a part of their destiny. Cheirologists talk about "the mark" on the palm of the hand that signifies the planning of such a traumatic exit, but that is not for me to discuss in this book. The reality is that, to date, I have still never met such a person. Suicide as an act of cultural tradition as in the act of Sepuku performed by the ancient Samurai, or as an act of self-defence (such as a soldier that takes his own life in order not to divulge military secrets) are a few examples of such deaths.

Some souls find their intended and carefully planned lives to be "just-too-much-to-handle" and choose suicide as an early exit. It is one of your carefully planned out choices at a planned crossroad in you life, but it is not the right one. When you arrive back at home you will appear before the Council of Elders where they will review your life with you. In this meeting you will be shown the choices you could have made instead of the suicide act and the outcome of the decision to persevere. There will be no anger towards you, no blame, and no recourse. They will be disappointed in you, but you will still feel their compassion and their love. The Creator will embrace you with his love and forgiveness, and you will feel no rejection. However (and you know this), there is always a recourse and repercussion. The lessons you had chosen to learn in the life where you exited that you had not learned in that specific lifetime (for example, say you chose to learn extreme grief from the loss of a very close sister, but you could not handle it and killed yourself instead) you will still need to learn and, therefore, you will have to come back sooner or later and learn the lesson all over again.

A School Called Earth

The difference however in the next life is that there may be some other harsh lessons to learn as well and this will make the next trip all the more difficult. It is like a college student who fails a first year subject but still gets to go to second year. In the second year, that student will have to manage all the second year subjects as well as carry over the first year subject that he failed – tough, isn't it?

The truth is that this "company car" you were given is not yours to destroy and you will have to settle for the "pool car" since there is no other vehicle in the fleet and you have a job to do. Don't complain when the car does not go as well as the last one and does not suit your personality – get the point?

Your planner guides would have warned you that this planet is tough (you will also have remembered past trips) and that you are taking on very tough lessons. Sometimes souls, like certain college students, choose to do first and second year in one and in some cases it just doesn't work and the task is too great to handle. You would have been warned and shown the signs, but souls have free will and sometimes they mirror the human trait of stubbornness and choose to tackle the lesson even though it is clear that the potential to pass is slim – it is called Free Will. But there is no punishment..

Here is one for the "church" to deal with. The Creator, as most faiths believe, is a GOD of unconditional love and not a GOD who wants to test the weakness of HIS creation. Why would any parent create a child that it loves, only to test the child's love for the parent and then punish the child when it fails the parent? Surely parents want the best for their children and love them unconditionally and forgive them for their disappointments? I am talking of loving parents and not the cruel primadonna types you see on TV soapies – pure love, loves unconditionally and forgives no matter what. Pure love wishes and wants for the best and does not set you up for failure so that it can punish its children. Pure love does not punish, but sometimes it may seem a bit cruel. Occasionally good parents have to execute a dose of "tough love". In certain situations, such as when certain weaker-willed teenagers are on the wrong path, parents are "forced" to get tough to ensure that their beloved children do not fall into traps set by lurking baddies. Take, for example, a teenager who is used to getting his own way. He has his own car, own spending allowance and starts to abuse drugs, alcohol and starts driving under the influence with other teenagers in the car. The parent, to help the teenager, may take away certain privileges such as a reduction of the spending allowance and car privileges (the car is only allowed to be used for going to campus - unless the teenager stops the abusive behaviour).

Those of you who have "grown-up" know that there is always a period of resentment towards the parent but, if handled carefully and with love and not rejection, the teenager will eventually grow up without causing a dreadful accident in the car while drunk, possibly destroying the lives of other innocents. (Go easy on this analogy – I have never been a parent – it's only an example). There is always the possibility that the teenager rebels to such an extent that he steals a car, gets drunk, has an accident and ends up hurting an innocent bystander. Even if this teenager fails miserably and goes to jail, a true loving parent will find forgiveness and still love their child.

In time, however, that teenager, as he matures and analyses his actions, will reflect on them, learn from them and try not fail again. So, too, does the soul get the opportunity to come back, learn that love is sometimes cruel in order for us to learn and in order for us to grow and become wiser adults who, in turn, can teach our own children. It's about the eternal lesson of cause and effect. We learn so that we can teach, and we teach so that we can learn more.

A School Called Earth

Past lives – why can't we remember?

The reason most people think they can't remember past lives is because we are not meant to remember how to remember. The reason some people get shown certain parts of their past lives or experience scenes in regressional therapy is because they were planned. When we need help our guides direct us to people and situations that can help us, and some of the help comes from memories of our past lives.

Ever met anyone who has no interest in the spirit world at all or simply does not believe in the afterlife at all? Guess what? They planned it! Some highly advanced souls I have met have no idea that they are highly advanced and have no interest in finding out why or what they were in previous lives.

I often get asked if past lives are not figments of our imaginations or clips from some movie our minds have subconsciously stored and now we believe that they are our own memories. Some religions even believe that talking about, or believing in, past lives is evil and that we will be damned to eternal hell for just thinking about it. Other religions, on the other hand, do believe in past lives or reincarnation but also believe that we upgrade from animal souls to humans or the other way around.

Does the Soul remember?

The simple answer is yes, it remembers all the lessons it learns, both at home and here on earth throughout all its lives. Each life on earth teaches us specific lessons that help the soul advance to the next soul level and to the next soul stage. A soul only has amnesia because we cannot focus on the future when we focus on the past. It is similar to people who do not grow because they constantly harp on past mistakes. It's not that history and past experiences are not necessary; on the contrary, they are vital. Lessons we have learnt become the wisdom we bring back to

A School Called Earth

this earth with us. It's the reason you no longer have the urge to murder, steal or rape in this life. You have somewhere, in one of your past lives, done it, been there and got the T-shirt. No one ever feels the need to buy another T-shirt exactly the same as the past one. The old one has fond memories, but there's no need to keep wearing it to remind you of the good times or lessons you learnt when you wore it.

John Edward (*One Last Time*, Piatkus, 1998) has the following brilliant analogy. "Jerry Maguire" is not aware that Tom Cruise was "Top Gun", but Tom Cruise knows he was both, and he – like the soul – will use both experiences to improve his next role.

This is what life is about. Much like a stage, this school I call earth allows us to perfect our performances, learn all the acting techniques we can and be the very best actors we can, before we move on to become scriptwriters (Planner Souls) or critics (Council of Elders) or the audience (The Creator). Sometimes when our acting goes a bit wrong, our producer (Guides) give us reminders of our past performances so that we can draw from our past learnings, draw from our last conquests or sometimes perfect a role that we did not do so well in.

So, when I get asked whether regression is right or wrong or even necessary, I have the following to say: it is ok to be shown our past only when it is completely necessary to save a life or the destiny of a soul on this earth. I do not do past life regression unless Uriall guides me to do so. Some humans have a morbid curiosity with certain past historic characters and want to know if they were famous. I have not met any significant historical character in any of my past-life regression sessions. I have met people who, in the past, have done some incredible things, but none that I have ever read about.

A School Called Earth

One of my own lives I can recall. Around 1645, I lived in Portugal, and was a poet/writer with a fair bit of local fame, but nothing that the world knows about and nothing that has changed history in any way. I wore a patch over my right eye which I lost in a sword duel whilst defending my honour. (In this duel, I killed a man for insulting the servant girl I loved. I was connected to royalty and should not have been fraternising with servants. But this again explains my current lack of respect for authority and especially royalty). I remember writing with a quill, and having spectators surround me waiting for my writings – snatched away before the ink was dry in order for these bemused friends to read my insights of the time. My name in that life was Luis too, and for some reason I am of Portuguese descent again, and in this life find myself writing again.

Strangely enough, I only have partial vision in my right eye - spooky. My mother has recently told me of a Portuguese poet with one eye who wrote great poetry by the name of Luis de Camoes. Perhaps there is a connection, but I am not drawn to finding out what or who this person was. I am not schooled in Portuguese history and I am not interested in reliving the past. I am a lot more interested in my future and how I can help and heal my fellow souls. I am sure that the wisdom I have does not come from this life alone; there is no way I know everything I know because of thirty eight years on Earth – clearly impossible.

I don't seek fame in this lifetime. Therefore, one of my lessons is not to let any fame of my writings go to my head. Furthermore, I believe that the ego is an obstacle that often prevents us from speaking the truth in case other people may not like what they hear. I, therefore, focus my life on building a sense of fulfilment from helping my fellow souls on the journey of discovery – discovering the truth and the truth of the Creator's Word. When, then, is past life regression ok? It's ok when it helps us as humans get affirmation and reassurance, especially if we are spiritually

A School Called Earth

lost. Sometimes we start feeling fears at the strangest times of our lives. I have always feared I would die at age thirty-three, and at that age I was diagnosed with a brain tumour. In one of my past life regressions in dream-state meditation, I discovered that in my two last lives I died at age thirty-three. In Vietnam as an American Soldier named Anibell Falcone, I got a bullet through the brain, which left me paralysed until I died of blood loss – a waste of a life. Before that, in 1932, I died at age thirty-three in a hail of gunfire as a New York gangster assassin. I thought I could walk away from it all as I had finally found love, but the head of the gang feared I would divulge bootlegging secrets to the police, and had the woman I loved and me, assassinated – live by the gun, die by the gun – a life wasted, but a tough lesson learned.

The soul has memory and sometimes it triggers the body to believe that the memories are real. So real that the body starts to gear up for a death around the time the soul last experienced death. My body went to the stage that it created a tumour – partly as soul memory, but mostly to remind me to wake up and not make the same mistakes again – cruel tough love, but, oh, what a wonderful love it is. The soul will sometimes give you a flashback as you daydream, as you sleep/dream at night or as part of a regression session. They are there to remind us of the lessons learned, so that we do not waste another life learning the same lesson again.

Soul memory is not the same as flesh memory. Soul memory lies in our spirit mind, whereas flesh memory lies in our genetic make-up. It's ok to have a fear of falling, spiders and snakes. Genetically our chromosomes carry memory; it's what keeps us alive and provides us with the "fight or flight" reactions. Through my documented case studies I have come to the understanding that these primitive emotions and survival instincts are not a part of our soul memory, but rather as a result of genetic conditioning.

A School Called Earth

There are some cases where, say, the fear of falling or getting eaten by sharks was created by a traumatic exit from a past life we lived. In these cases past-life regression is a path to healing.

But all of this said, it important for you to live in the "present". The past and the future do not exist in the present. The past consists of memories, either good or bad and the future consists of imagination of what life could be like or the consequences of our actions in the future. There is nothing you can do about the past and even less about the future (I don't mean planning, because planning becomes your roadmap for a happier "present" in the future). I mean that living with the unhappy or happy memories of the past and wishing you had them over again, leaves you with stress because you don't have it in the present and, furthermore, can do nothing in the present to recreate or fix it. Also, worrying about what could possibly go wrong in the future will cause you stress because there is nothing you can do about it in the present moment. There is a gap between the past and the present and between the future and the present. This gap is what causes your stress and your stress is what makes you unhappy. Right here and right now, while you are reading this book, everything is fine. You are not thinking, you are absorbing the information, and perhaps later you will think about what you have read. As soon as you stop reading and start thinking about the future or the wrongs of the past, you start to stress and again become unhappy. So, do yourself a huge favour, learn to live in the here and now all the time. Catch yourself thinking about any negative thoughts about your past (or what could have happened in your past life/lives) or your future, and stop yourself from thinking those thoughts. Your mind, the part of you that thinks, is only your body's brain thinking (just one of your many organs, however important science may think it is). It is not your soul. Your soul does not think; it feels, senses and experiences. Your thinking and the way you have defined yourself through your thinking is an illusion created by your brain, making you believe that because you think, you are. This is a lie, and a huge one at that. If you define yourself through your thinking, then you are caught up in your ego self and the ego self is the cause of all misery in this world. Do not define yourself by the illusion of intelligence and worldly wealth and beauty. Define yourself by your senses. Live in the here and now, and you will find that your life will soon be without stress.

Try this one for your sanity, "I feel, therefore I am". In the now I am all that I am and this means that forever I am what I feel. Feels good, doesn't it?

Every lesson bears a gift you have asked for.
Every challenge you seek comes bearing gifts for you to pick.
Accept the gift and understand the lesson.

Cruel lives, traumatic death situations – Why do we need to suffer?
Many of my clients ask why we need to live in suffering or experience trauma when we die. Here are some of Uriall's comments on the subject.

Suffering and trauma are some of the hardest lessons the soul has to endure. As souls we have many lessons to learn and cruelty, fear and suffering are part of the balance of other lessons such as fame, bravery and joy. We have all learned, or will still learn, them. That is why it's so important that, as humans, we show compassion and caring for our fellow man. We are all interconnected and caring and compassion means a love for the Creator and all of His Creation which, of course, includes our fellow man and us. Remember, for every action there is an equal and active reaction. Sow pain and one day you will reap it. Rape or murder and one day you will be raped or murdered – it's your choice, your free will.

A School Called Earth

Traumatic death situations – does a soul really need to feel what it is like to get eaten by a shark? No, and here is my interpretation based on my experience. In a skydiving exercise, I saw a soul leave a body, wave me goodbye and go home. The body became lifeless, pulled the chords, the chute turned into a roman candle (wrapped around itself) and the body plummeted to earth. When we landed we found our friend dead. Diagnosis – he died from the impact – it must have been traumatic – the family really felt grief and the thought of Johnny fearing and waiting for the impact made it worse. I have not spoken to the parents (serious churchgoers who believe that I am possessed by the devil), but if they only knew that Johnny passed peacefully and quickly and did not wait for the bodily impact before leaving this earth they would feel better about his passing.

In one of my past lives around 1520, my soul hovered over my body as I watched it get eaten by sharks as the ship I sailed in got shot-up by a pirate ship and sank. I watched in anger, but I felt no pain. It was not long before the pulling sensation began and I was led to our beautiful home. No pain, no trauma, just a frustration at an early exit, which I later realised I had planned. In that life I left behind my wife and kids to discover new worlds. I left behind my soulmate, who mourned me until she died of a broken heart. I could have spent a life loving her and being loved by her but, instead, I wasted a life chasing a dream. We do tend to learn some traumatic lessons with our soulmates as partners.

And now one of my favourite questions…

A soulmate – does everyone have one?
This is always an amusing subject. Yes, you will one day have a soulmate, pretty much the way you find a spouse on this earth. Some of my clients always find this a tough one to swallow, especially if they have not found "true love" in this lifetime.

A School Called Earth

The way it works, though, is pretty logical and straightforward. Children don't marry, teenagers shouldn't but do, young adults do and that's ok, adults do and by then it should work out, old folk do but it is for different reasons than that of the teenagers. Probably an over simplified analogy, but there's a similar pattern with souls.

As Souls progress through the ladders of spiritual Soul maturity, they start to yearn for a partner. In nature there are two of everything. The Creator consists of two; Yin and Yang – two; good and evil – two; husband and wife – two. So two souls eventually enter into a sacred long-term partnership that resembles a marriage. From my experience it is only from the mature soul stage that we start to partner up with another soul – what we as humans call a "soulmate" – an eternal partner. Up until this stage we live in soul groups. We partner any of our soul classmates. We pick them as brothers, sisters, fathers, mothers, aunts, uncles, friends, acquaintances and even enemies. Here is an irony; Bush and Bin Laden belong to the same group of mature souls that incarnate on this earth. They have chosen to be enemies in this life and several other past ones. Makes you wonder – spooky. (By the way – I have yet to see an advanced soul in a presidential role – the oldest souls I have seen in world leaders are in the former South African presidents who, strangely enough, belong to the same mature soul group as well – Nelson Mandela and FW de Klerk).

Free will again allows us to be closer to some souls than others. It is not that we dislike any of the souls in our group, because we don't dislike anyone in the spirit world. We just prefer certain of our classmates because they complement us as soulmates. Eventually, as souls mature, we find a soulmate with whom we enjoy incarnating as a spouse and, eventually, we will enter into a soul marriage on the other side. Usually, by the time you have reached this level, you will come to earth as an advanced soul and spend some interesting and challenging times together.

A School Called Earth

However, as souls enter the highly advanced (old soul stage) and become closer to the God Source or the Creator's energy, they start to lose their need for individuality and, therefore, no longer need to be a part of a soul partnership. As highly advanced souls we will have the opportunity to be absorbed back into the Creator's energy, or take on a permanent role such as becoming a part of an angel group.

As a soul that is fiercely independent, my soul named Michaelilu is part of the Michaelilu group. My soul is a primary teacher and protector of souls back at home. On earth I have loved, and fallen in love, several times. The women I have loved have all been wonderful partners and I have learnt a great deal from each and every one of them. One of my students back home, Delfina, an entertainer, has always been a close friend on the other side and she has felt the same way about me. We became partners on earth and our time together was filled with love and happiness. We parted as friends and, one day, we will be friends on the other side. She has taught me some wonderful lessons in this lifetime, even though they have not all been easy. We were together on this earth for as long as it took both of us to learn a certain lesson. Once the lesson was learnt it was time to part ways so we could learn other lessons that we would not have learnt together. Just because we are part of a soul group in the spirit world does not mean we have to spend time together on this school ground.

It may or may not be unusual to take on a student as a spouse, but as there are only three souls left in my group back home (the others have either progressed to the next level similar to that of the elders or remained in a level behind because they are slower learners) and the other two are soulmates, leaving me to play odd one out. So I have not yet entered into a sacred marriage contract back at home and that's okay, because the right soul will eventually come along if it is required for me to experience such a lesson.

A School Called Earth

Even though we may not be in the same classroom level as souls, (we start as a group of roughly fifty souls per classroom that form a part of main groups that make a cluster of about one thousand souls) and the fact that the higher we progress the more classrooms we teach, still makes us a part of a large cluster unit, as I explained in an earlier chapter. Therefore, our soulmate, as far as I can interpret Uriall's explanations, come from either the initial group of fifty, or from somewhere in our cluster where we have met, taught, been taught and experienced time with a specific soul with whom we resonate and make a perfect learning partnership.

Animal Souls

Do animals have souls? A resounding yes is the answer. I know that some biblical and religious writings disagree, but I only tell what I can see.

Animals, especially pets, exist on the other side. From what I can remember, there are fewer species back home than on earth, but that is because this planet needs all the animals as a part of the biosphere's evolutionary and survival cycle. The earth needs predators that eat herbivores to stop them from eating all the vegetation as they increase in number. For example, on the other side I have only seen large cats chasing buck as a game. They have no need for food on the other side so no one needs to die so the other can survive.

Animal souls are also different from the souls of humans. These souls are softer energies. One could say that they are a smaller size and made up of more simplistic energy. These souls have a healing ability. They are highly compassionate and thus they choose to come to earth as pets, which become our companions and often have the uncanny ability of healing us in grief periods.

A School Called Earth

Do we upgrade from animals?
No. Animal souls are created as energies that incarnate as animals. They, too, can grow in wisdom and knowledge, but these energies remain as animal souls. Human beings are made up in the image of souls. Yes, we do have appendages that souls do not but, because we have not yet learnt to progress in energy shifting, we need the appendages to help us get around.

Can we incarnate as animals?
Before your soul incarnates into human form it sometimes, but very seldom, uses an animal's body to experience the birth process and the Earth dimension. This is a carefully managed process and the angels and planners are always nearby to assist. Souls will incarnate most often into animals such as birds and dolphins and certain types of apes. The soul will only spend a short period in the animal and then pass the body back to its rightful animal soul owner. "Human" souls are usually braver than that and so they mostly incarnate directly into human. At first, these humans will live fairly subsistent lives, where they learn to adapt to the earth dimension and learn to slowly manage and control the human body. All first time incarnations will involve the soul in simple lives where the lessons are physical and focus is on primal lessons.

Can animal souls become human?
No, as previously mentioned these souls are of a different kind to the human soul and have no need for earthly or other planetary incarnations and lessons.

Picking a life and a body for this journey
Here is an analogy. Your body is like a company car. Your brain is the engine and your soul is the driver. Your destination is from Cape to Cairo. Know this much. You will end up in Cairo. You can get there on your own

A School Called Earth

fuel and even help others get there too but get there you will, even if it means getting towed there or put on the back of a recovery truck. You have many routes to Cairo and each one will have different scenery and different experiences. The route you take is your own and up to your own judgement. You would do well to remember this; Ferraris don't do well on a 4x4 course and 4x4s are not good at breakneck speeds. Choose your route well and use your past driving experiences to help you cope with the road's challenges.

Our life is similar. You join a company and get a company car. A Mazda is not what you really think you want but that's what you have and so you take care of the body or your car will look like a scrap heap before you get to Cairo. You can add mag-wheels and go-faster stripes. It may look great, but it's still a Mazda. As long as mag-wheels make you happy, add them but don't do it to impress the neighbours because somewhere out there is a Ferrari and no matter how zooty your Mazda is, people generally are still more impressed by the Ferrari. Only the driver and other occupants are grateful for the Mazda. Remember, if the only way you can be admired is via your looks, it will only be a matter of time before there is either a new model or more attractive vehicle that will take attention away from you and, unless you have occupants that love the inner beauty of your vehicle, you will be left high and dry and so very lonely to admire your own reflection. Be careful what you wish for!

The engine is another story. You really could have done with a smooth V6, but a small 1300 is all you were given. Cairo is a long way away, so drive carefully and don't exhaust the little motor and be careful of abusing it or adding additives to make it go faster. Also we know that a great driver (Like Schumacher) driving a Mazda could probably beat a granny in a Ferrari around a racetrack, purely because of driving ability and previous racing experience. You don't need a Ferrari to be intelligent,

A School Called Earth

caring and sympathetic to people in need. Anyway, a Ferrari is a selfish vehicle because it can only seat two, yet a Mazda MPV can seat 8. It depends on what is important to you - status or family carrying capacity? Be careful what you wish for!

And then comes the important factor, the driver. Some of us are better drivers than others. So are some souls better drivers of the bodies they have been given. How do you become a better driver? You practise and go to driving school or racing school if you so wish. Some of us get faster or bigger cars than others. Drivers are not always happier in a Ferrari, because it may be fast but it's not comfortable and draws far too much attention.

So, those of you who are disappointed with the body you have, need to know this: **YOU PICKED YOUR BODY AND ITS RACE, SHAPE AND COMPOSITION!** You also chose your brain and its capacity. So stop blaming God or your current or past lives. You chose this body because it has taught you lessons you needed to learn. Somewhere in your past you have had the perfect body. In that life you were probably admired and loved, but you were most probably a user of others, and used your beauty to reach certain goals with ease. I have yet to find a highly advanced soul that is cover-girl beautiful. They do not need that outer beauty. They have an inner beauty that makes them magnetic and attractive. Advanced souls know how to be attractive without the physicality of it. So be grateful for what you have and be careful of what you wish for!

Give people a lift in this life. Remember the parable of the Good Samaritan. You do not have to give everyone a lift, but helping others gives you much self-fulfilment and you never know when you run into trouble and you may have a mechanic onboard. Don't go about picking up mechanics for a just-in-case emergency. Do so because you want to

A School Called Earth

help and not because you have to help. Everything you do in life should be because you want to and not because you have to, or feel bound by duty. As my friend Colleen Joy-Page wrote; why does an apple tree make apples? Because it just does! (*My Life as an Apple tree*). It's not for the farmer or to feed the birds or to impress passers-by. It's just because an apple tree makes apples.

And in making apples, or doing what you do best because that's who you are, you become the best you can be, both for your soul's destiny, and for the good of the Creator. In doing the best you can we all benefit because, by doing so the collective whole grows and we all become better for it. Thanks to all of you that just are and do what you do because that's what you do.

If you do something that makes you unhappy, or live a role that makes you stress, then you are plain crazy. Stop the craziness. You have a choice. You always have a choice. The choice is simple. Stop doing what makes you unhappy and do what makes you happy, or just do nothing and accept what you are doing and stop thinking about it, because it's the thinking about the situation you are in that makes you unhappy. Whatever you do in your life, do it with all your passion and love, or don't do it at all. Doing nothing is as good as doing anything, as long as you do it to the best of your ability.

A good man is an evil man's teacher.
A good man is an evil man's student.
Both are the same and both are required for a classroom to exist.

Life Paths – The Lessons and Free Will
Have you noticed that all people are different yet in many ways similar?

A School Called Earth

It's because as souls we have several life paths and master-learning paths. I know many have written about a soul's destiny and have gone into infinite detail about this topic. I have simplified this in my own way and, again, remember I don't know everything – even though my students often think so. I have broken down the soul's journey into seven main categories, which I call seven life paths. These are not set in concrete so, if you are a policewoman it does not necessarily mean that your soul is on a protector life path. I have generalised the categories based on my case study research. Here are the seven life paths and the type of roles you "often" find in our modern society.

1. **Warrior**
   - Soldier
   - Politician
   - Activist

2. **Teacher**
   - School teacher
   - Preacher
   - Minister
   - Pioneer

3. **Healer**
   - Doctor and medical staff
   - Spiritual healer and alternative medicine practitioner
   - Traditional healer, witchdoctor etc
   - Minister, priests and religious worker

4. **Nurturer/Caretaker**
   - Nurse in paediatric ward
   - Mother

- Foster home parent
- Ambulance worker
- Conservationist
- Animal worker
- Forester

5. **Protector**
    - Parent
    - Social worker
    - Policeman
    - Fireman
    - Bodyguard
    - Security guard
    - Soldier

6. **Creator**
    - Artist
    - Scientist
    - Inventor
    - Farmer
    - Biologist

7. **Entertainer**
    - Dancer
    - Actor
    - Musician
    - Clown

Once, I asked the Creator for Strength – He gave me difficulties to make me strong.

Then, I asked him for Wisdom - He gave me tough problems to learn to solve.

I asked him for Courage – He gave me dangers to overcome.

Finally, I asked Him for Love - He gave me people with challenges to help.

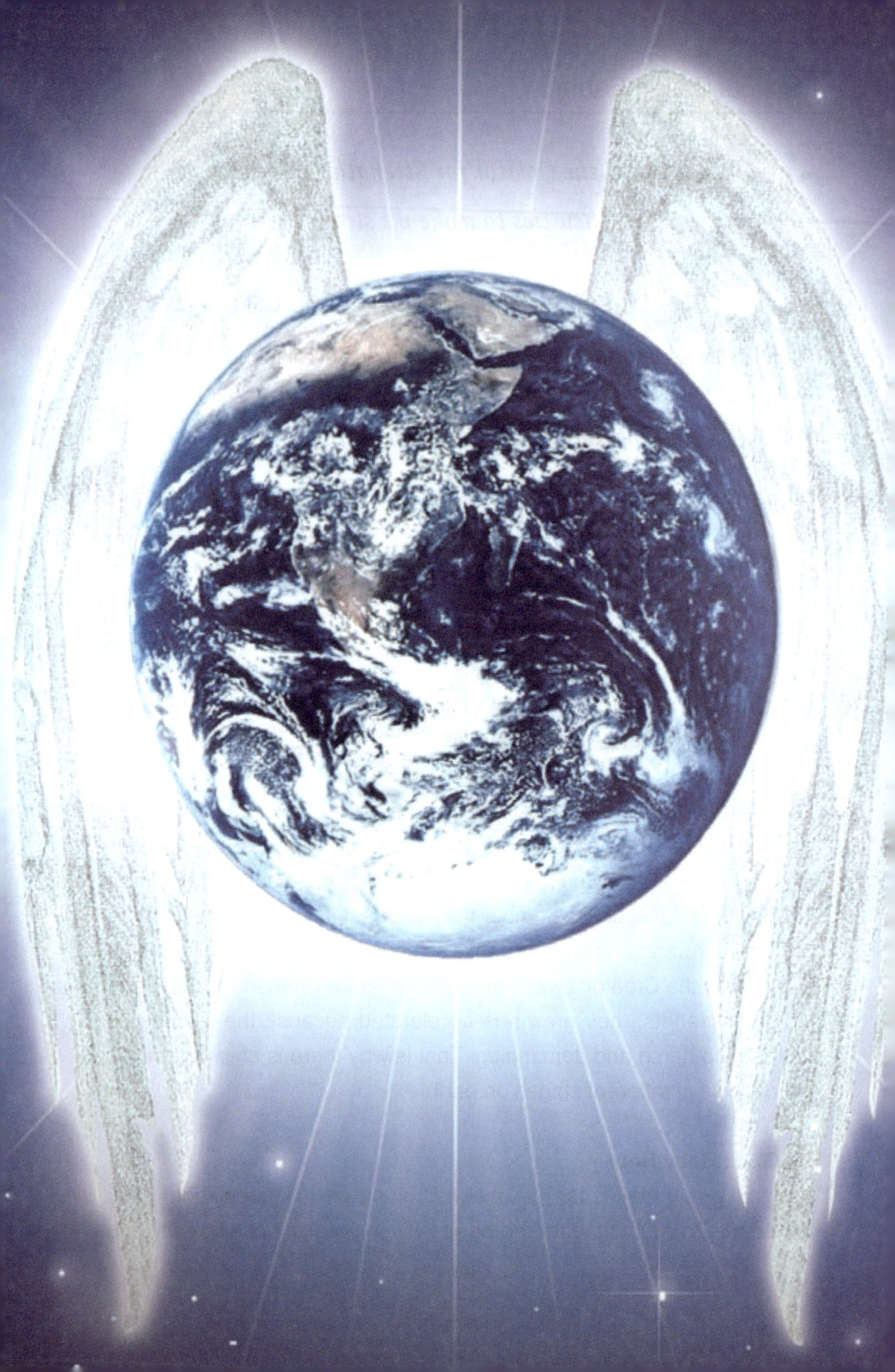

CHAPTER 4
Soul advancement

Soul stages

The following is information from my client case studies, guidance from Uriall and what I see. Souls mature through a series of stages. Each stage is not a life, because you have many lessons to learn at each stage. Most souls only take on one or two lessons in their youth. As the soul matures, so it may take on a few more lessons at a time. Generally only the old souls do that because it sometimes takes many lives to learn one lesson such as overcoming prejudice.

As I previously mentioned, souls do not advance from animal to human. Animals have a different energy to humans, and their souls play a different role altogether to that of the human soul. They have their own place at home and do not have the soul structures that human souls have.

Souls go through five main stages before they stop reincarnating on this earth. (There are seven stages but I will only discuss the 1st five). The stages are: Baby Soul, Young Soul, and Mature Soul, Old Soul and finally Advanced Soul. Remember this is not set in concrete but is more my own interpretation of our progress as souls. Souls mature at home as they grow in the Creator's wisdom and love. As they reincarnate on earth and other planets, their growth is accelerated because the lessons on earth are so harsh and demanding. That is why there is always a mixed bag of souls at different stages on earth.

STAGE 1: Baby Soul

This soul group makes for just over half of the world's population. Baby souls come to earth to learn the basics. They live lives of simplicity and

A School Called Earth

often live lives that centre on survival. In human form on earth they live in rural surroundings and live off the earth. We often feel sympathy for these souls, though we shouldn't, because we have been there ourselves. Compassion and empathy for souls in these harsh living conditions is the proper emotion to have. Emotions without actions are, however, futile and as souls on this earth we are bound by the Creator's duty to care for them. I do not mean sell everything you own and become a social worker, but when you do come across these souls you should give a little, because a little, to them, goes a long way.

The lessons that these souls come to learn are as follows:
- Basic instincts
- Survival
- Fear
- Procreation and the fears surrounding the actions
- What is right and wrong
- What constitutes a good life

These souls will either become the victim or the aggressor. They will get the opportunity to do both. For the pure baby soul the hardest task is to manage this primitive, dense human body with very strong survival instincts. The "fight or flight" emotions are very difficult for the young soul to manage and they often make big mistakes. These souls often find themselves in situations as the murderer or rapist or their victims. Because these souls are still in large school groups, back at home, they tend to belong to a large community and family-like structures on earth where the whole soul group can spend time on earth together. Travelling around the rural parts of Brazil and Africa I have come across many such soul groups.

A School Called Earth

Sometimes, when a man is thirsty, it is better to give him a drink of water, than to take pride in teaching him how to dig a well.

Then after he has drunk from your cup, you could help him dig.

Or else he can die of thirst before he can learn how to dig for water.

STAGE 2: Young Soul
This group accounts for about 25% of the world's population. Young souls can be either highly conservative in their views or highly reckless. There are often no in-betweens in this group. As humans, the soul starts to become more active leading them to look for religion as a way of life. To them, any religion they start off with they will end up with. They do not question the faith they are in but follow it blindly. Please be aware that religion and spirituality are not the same but often religion is used to attain spirituality. This soul group is still young in certain primitive instinctual actions and in a male body the need to hunt is still there. In female bodies the soul has a huge urge to procreate and raise a family from a young age (not to be confused with the nurturer soul).

Young souls are often happy when surrounded by many other similar Souls and work well with others. They are happy in large groups and have very little desire to stand out and be counted. Although they may get caught up with chasing the luxuries of the modern world, they do not do it for status, but for a basic survival need. Many of my clients with petty criminal convictions happen to belong to this group.

STAGE 3: Mature Soul

Uriall calls these souls actors and drama queens. As humans they have a need for power and drama in their lives and are drawn to conflict situations. These souls are also often drawn to vanity and you see them manifest this in the way they spend endless hours focusing on outer beauty or fighting for authority and position. These souls have an amazing amount of energy but spend it in chasing their own goals. They only seem to help others when it furthers their own cause. No need to worry, if you are reading this book, you are not one of them. Mature souls have no need for spirituality and if they did start off in a religion, they will only stay there for fear of eternal damnation. Mature souls have no interest in their own soul progress and are focused on managing the body. As souls have no vanity, the only reason these souls appear to be vain is because they have not learnt to manage the human body and brain completely and thus give in to the body's need for these earthly attainments. The body is fear-based, and fear is a difficult human emotion for mature souls to manage.

These souls often still indulge in religion and religious acts, but this is mostly for show or because of a "Fear of God". This stage in soul progression is never easy as the soul wisdom conflicts with the body's need. As these people get older and their death come closer they often become quite critical of their past in this life and question the time they have wasted being materialistic and futile. Most souls take as many as ten human lifetimes to progress past this stage, because this world we live in rewards the powerful, rich and famous. Mature souls know exactly how to extract the best from the world to suit their own means.

A School Called Earth

The Creator is the centre of the universe,
The good man's reward, the bad man's refuge

STAGE 4: Old Soul

This means you. You would not be reading this book if you were not an old soul – unless you are reading this book to prove to yourself that I, and all others like me, are complete nuts or frauds.

Old souls are reaching the end of their earthly incarnations. These souls do not always have easy lives as the lessons at this stage become emotionally tough. Lessons that you are likely to learn are of high emotional content and the soul gets to learn wisdom through these processes. Old souls have no interest in taking it easy. We all wish for wealth, beauty, peace and popularity, but no one has become wise without struggle.

Old souls all seek spiritual balance and wisdom from all others. They realise that they can learn from every situation, and start seeking wisdom (not intelligence or academia) from a very young age. They are often very profound and have sincerity about them that no other soul stage other than the advanced soul has. They very seldom do things without taking others into consideration and they have a profound healing ability, manifested by the way they help and guide others. Many of these souls have no idea that they are old, advanced beings, but they all have the gift of intuition and wisdom. Please note that I have said wisdom and not intelligence. I have met many an old soul that would not be considered to be intelligent and of a high IQ. Rather, they have very high EQ, otherwise known as emotional intelligence.

Old souls find that religion no longer has the ultimate truth, and therefore they question for the sake of knowledge and wisdom. As humans, these souls will only use religion if it can really help others and, although on the surface they may seem religious, they are in actual fact very spiritual.

All old souls have a close relationship with their guides. They may call this relationship by many different names, but in essence they all have a very loud inner voice or spiritual voice guidance. These souls often appear "by mistake" at the right place at the right time and seem to save the situation almost as if it were planned. It is exactly so. Not all old souls are aware of their roles, but this is by prior consent with the planners and master guides before incarnation on earth. These old souls very often take menial earthly tasks and I have often seen them working in jobs such as ambulance workers, crisis councillors, waiters and fire fighters. The world would question this but these souls take on roles where they can help others in dire need without the flamboyant need for high drama and reward. Their tasks often go unseen, but they touch people in a profound and spiritual way that is often never thought about or considered to be miraculous. You will almost always see these souls in life paths that are difficult with harsh lessons, but most importantly, you will find these souls working with people in a basic and simplistic way.

Physically, these are not the most beautiful looking people you will meet. They never judge others, yet they are always judged themselves. These souls choose harsh lessons, often early on in life so that in learning they can guide, teach and influence others to grow spiritually and therefore advance to their next soul stage. These souls, however, have an inner beauty that makes them hugely attractive as beings. Their light shines on forever in our memories, long after we have forgotten their names and faces. Stop looking for angels out there – they are amongst you in the form of old souls and they are here to help.

A School Called Earth

*Please take your passing on seriously.
However, if you laugh on the way to your execution,
don't be alarmed when lesser Souls call you crazy.*

STAGE 5: Advanced Soul

When the student is ready the master will come, really applies to these fascinating souls. There are less than 10, 000 of these souls on earth, and they also vary in levels of advancement. Ultimately, when they reach enlightenment, they stop reincarnating and go back into the energy of the Creator. More importantly, they do not come around often, and are here for four specific tasks namely

- To teach enlightenment
- To change the course of the world's direction
- To learn how to use the body/mind of a human being so that, as future master guides, planners and angels they can connect with our minds and thus guide us in the Creator's wisdom
- To heal others

That's all I'm prepared to write on this soul level. You'll know these characters because you have met them. Their words and actions change your life forever. Their memories are never lost in your mind and you will never forget them. Sometimes they (The Enlightened ones) are considered great prophets and teachers and often they are both revered and hated by people. Jesus, Buddha, The Dalai Llama, Mother Theresa, Sai Baba are but a few of these people the world knows. Many other highly advanced ones are less known to the greater world, figures like Nelson Mandela, Michael Newton, Sylvia Brown, and John Edward.

A School Called Earth

Still others are completely unknown to the world. They can be the guy that stopped when you broke down on that quiet highway in the middle of nowhere and touched you with his/her ability to heal your soul, or wonderful teachers of spirituality and life paths. People such as my dear friend and mentor Dr. D Lilley or Colleen Joy Page who, on a daily basis, either heals you physically or puts you on such a spiritual path that your soul probably grows more in one lifetime than it has in all the previous lives put together. They do this as a matter of fact – no airs, no graces no reward other than their own fulfilment derived from their ability to give of themselves unconditionally and without thought or prejudice in any form whatsoever. I thank our Creator for these wonderful beings of enlightenment. Where would we be without them?

A NEW STAGE: Indigos (A different species of soul)
I call them a different species because these souls or spiritual beings have never been on this planet before. This soul is here on earth for a very specific task. Much has been written about Indigo souls, but much of it is very far fetched.

Firstly I would like to set this straight for the record. There is no indigo in them. Indigo, azure, cobalt or dark blue purple is the colour of old or advanced Souls. These indigo Souls that the world is referring to are, in actual fact, a tangerine colour. They have no layers, no primary and secondary colours. They are tangerine throughout.

What makes them so different? These highly evolved souls belong to a group similar to the angels. They are not angels, but have similar characteristics in that they all have collective group tasks. These souls are here for a very specific task. They are here to "fix" this planet's destructive path.

A School Called Earth

Indigos started incarnating on this earth as early as the seventies. In the beginning they were just a few and they came to earth in order for the planet to start understanding how to deal with such beings. Most of them were severely misunderstood, and most of those early incarnations have left the planet. In the eighties the number almost doubled. By the nineties, one in every thousand souls was an indigo. By 2007 one in every one hundred is an indigo. These souls have the gift of high intuition and have the ability to learn as a collective whole. As one wises up, they all do. They have little worldly ambition or the need for worldly possessions. They seem not to cope with their lives and find the way of the world to have nothing of interest to them. Like the rest of the incarnating souls they have amnesia of who they are and why they are here. The task is very specific and will start in 2007 and come to a global consciousness by 2012. They will, by then, be given the gift of sight and will be able to see the spirit world as a natural action.

Many clients bring their children to my practice due to behavioural disorders. Many of these children suffer from anxiety, stress and other traumatic problems caused by our crazy society and pressure put on these innocents from a young age. Many of these kids are just plain indigos, and are misunderstood because they are not like us. The problem is not the child. The problem is that we, as adults, do not know how to interact with indigo souls.

Here are some typical characteristics that indigo souls portray. Not all these conditions portray indigos and not all indigos have all these characteristics, but they serve as a guideline for those of you who have children that are indigos or who, as children, battled to be understood because of your characteristics that appeared abnormal to everyone but you.

A School Called Earth

Indigos are often:
- Without an overwhelming need to become someone important
- Don't want to grow up to be anything – they just are who they are
- Bored by humans and activities that the human race enjoys such as sport, war, politics etc
- Have no need to plan their future unless it makes their parents feel comforted by the fact that they will be okay
- Overactive with wild imaginations and the ability to understand stuff that adults are unable to
- Have the wisdom that takes most humans an entire "old soul" life to reach
- Have an intuitive, psychic nature without knowing it or questioning where it comes from
- Never been on this earth before and therefore seem to be naive in many ways. They have very little need for worldly possessions. They seek knowledge only attained through interaction and not learned in books
- Seem to be hyperactive and restless – due to an inability to cope or function with our society's norms and traditions
- With a little guidance these souls get a sense of purpose. Medication or drugs of any sort are not needed! Many of the children that come and see me take themselves off drugs such as Ritalin and go on to living perfectly balanced worldly lives
- They care very little about the things I write about in this book, because they are here for a very specific purpose and have no time to waste on things that their souls have an intimate understanding of

For indigo children schools, churches and any place run by authoritarians are places of training and not wisdom or spiritual growth and so these

A School Called Earth

souls find going to such places boring and worthless. They will lack concentration and motivation and we all know how society treats those who do not excel or at least try and conform to our ancient processes of teaching.

They are here on this earth for a very specific reason. This will all come to light in about 2012 where their collective energy will come together and help fix this planet's destructive path. By 2014 they will, pretty much, run the planet probably without knowing that they do. That is all I can share on the subject of these beautiful creatures of our divine Creator.

If, however, you want to learn more I highly recommend the following books:

- The Indigo Children – Lee Carroll & Jan Tober – Hay House.
- Edgar Cayce on Understanding the Indigo Children – Peggy Day & Susan Gale – A.R.E Press.

Fig 2: Indigo Spirit and Soul

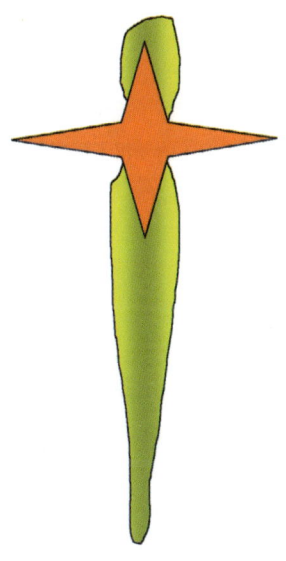

A School Called Earth

Both cats and dogs make loving pets.
Just don't try and get your cat to play fetch
Or
He may just fetch your favourite goldfish!

CREATION OF SOULS

BABY SOUL

YOUNG SOUL

TEACHING OR HEALING ROUTE

NURTURING OR HEALING ROUTE

MATURE SOUL

OLD SOUL

ADVANCED SOUL

SECONDARY GUIDE STAGE

PRIMARY GUIDE STAGE

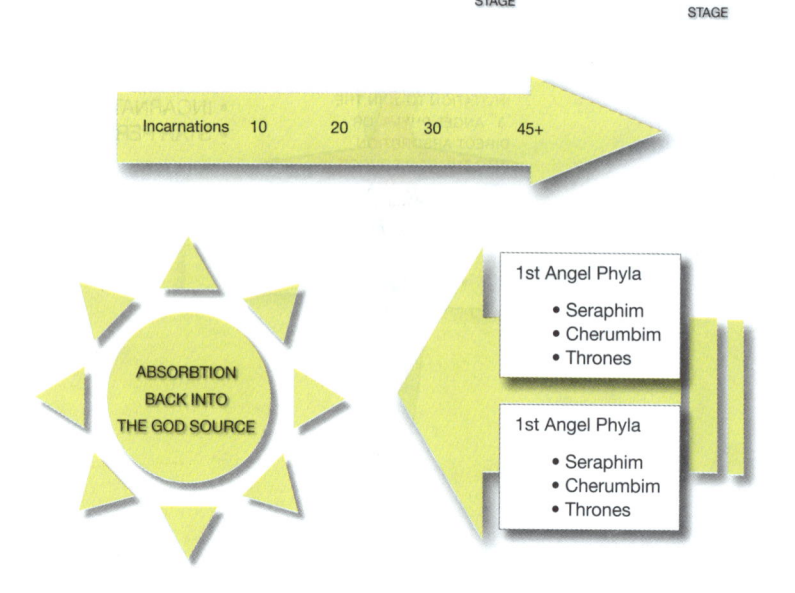

Incarnations   10   20   30   45+

ABSORBTION BACK INTO THE GOD SOURCE

1st Angel Phyla
- Seraphim
- Cherumbim
- Thrones

1st Angel Phyla
- Seraphim
- Cherumbim
- Thrones

A School Called Earth

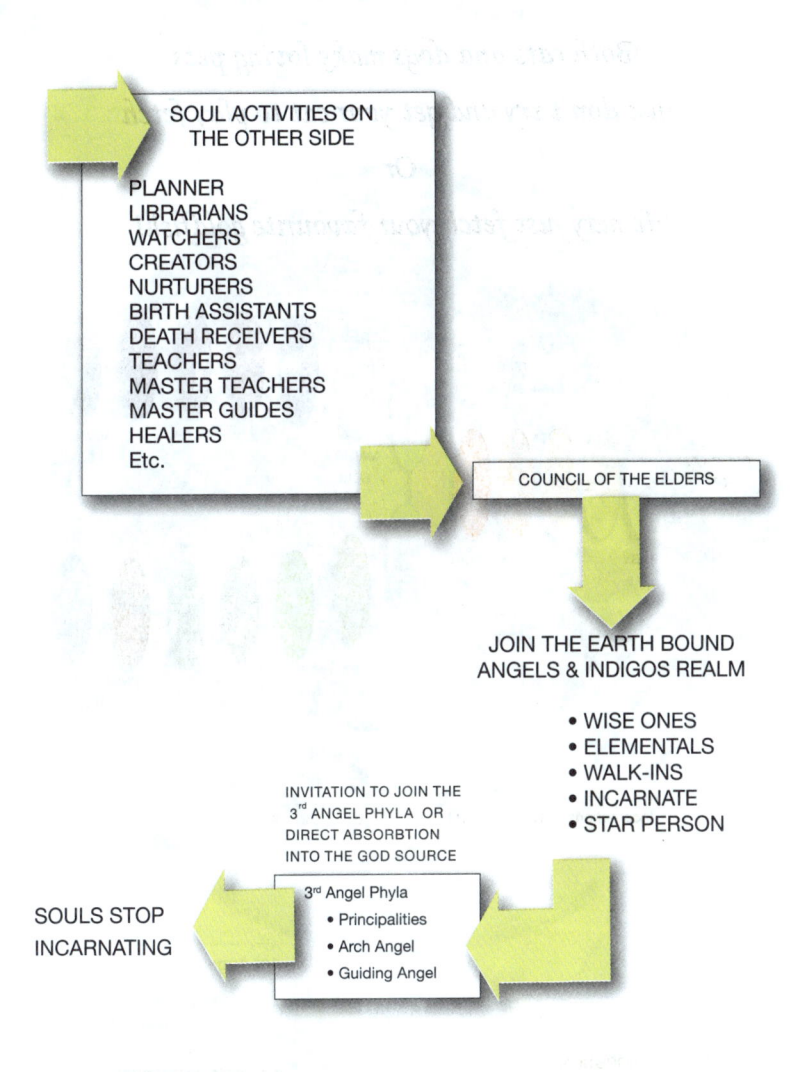

SOUL ACTIVITIES ON THE OTHER SIDE

PLANNER
LIBRARIANS
WATCHERS
CREATORS
NURTURERS
BIRTH ASSISTANTS
DEATH RECEIVERS
TEACHERS
MASTER TEACHERS
MASTER GUIDES
HEALERS
Etc.

COUNCIL OF THE ELDERS

JOIN THE EARTH BOUND ANGELS & INDIGOS REALM

- WISE ONES
- ELEMENTALS
- WALK-INS
- INCARNATE
- STAR PERSON

INVITATION TO JOIN THE 3rd ANGEL PHYLA OR DIRECT ABSORBTION INTO THE GOD SOURCE

3rd Angel Phyla
- Principalities
- Arch Angel
- Guiding Angel

SOULS STOP INCARNATING

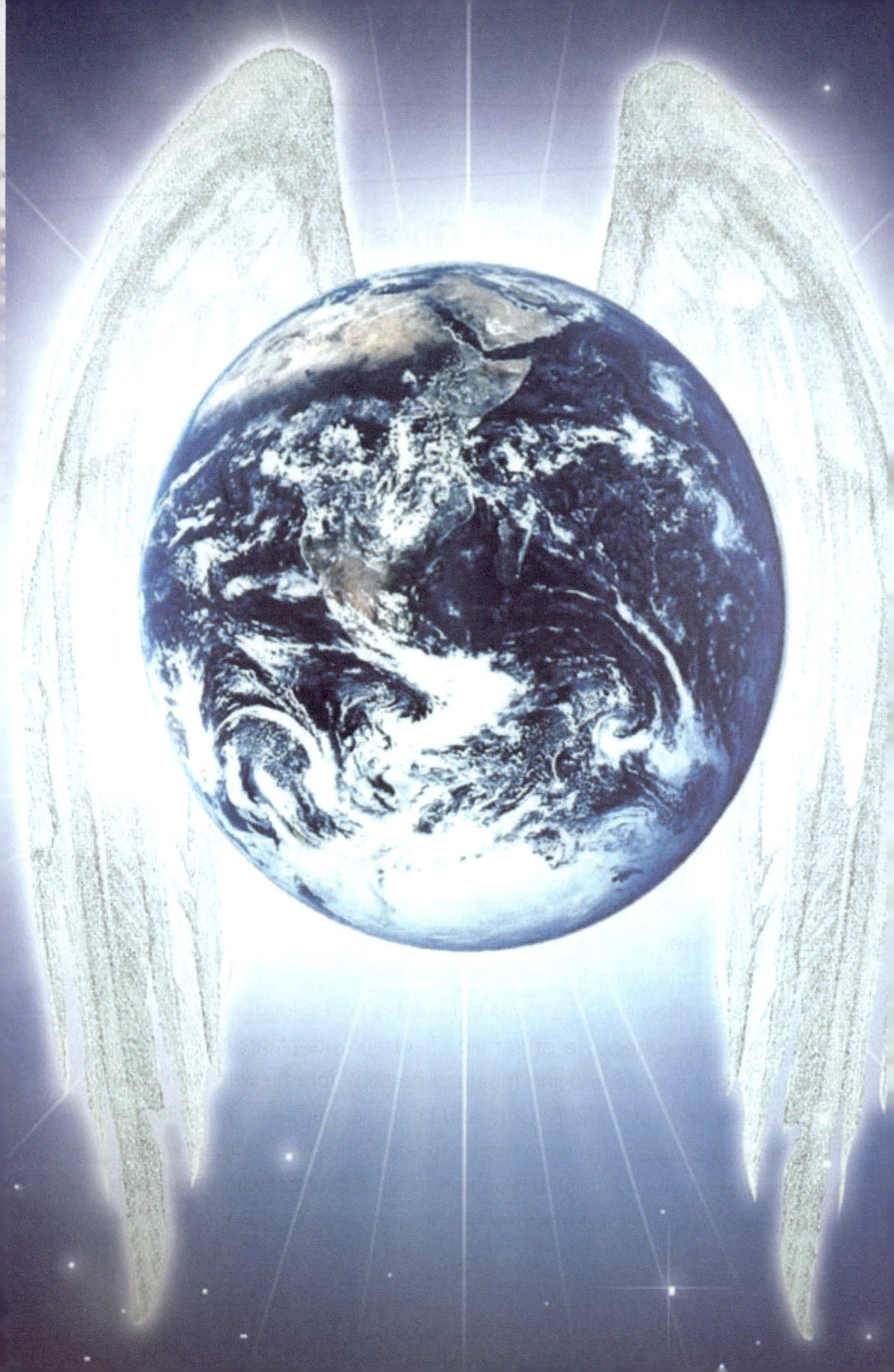

CHAPTER 5
Spirit Guides, Spirits, Ghosts and Angels

What is a spirit guide?
A spirit guide is a soul that has advanced to, at least, the advanced soul level. There are different types of guides and sometimes guidance comes from more than one guide at the same time. There are three types of guides and they are not to be mistaken for angels. They three types of guides are known as master, primary and secondary guides.

Primary guides
All of us have at least one primary guide. Primary guides are assigned to us in a sacred contract we make on the other side and are with us from the time we enter into a body on this earth. Their role is to be our main guardian, guide and teacher. They ensure that we stay on our destined and planned path and they form the core of our soul's direction and consciousness.

Our primary guides are more advanced than us. They would have learnt the lessons we still have to learn in order to be able to guide us. Primary guides are the link between us, the planners, the angels and the master guides. They will ask the other side to assist when they cannot and will go back and forth to ask for intervention should our souls be on the wrong path or be in dire need of a miracle. Miracles take a lot of planning and counter-planning because of karmic effect and pre-planned contracts. Imagine your spouse is dying (planned death before he was born) and because of your love and prayers and because, perhaps, you still have not learnt the lesson you were meant to learn, the other side allows him to live. Before you incarnated, you had made a contract with the person you would have married after the death of your spouse. Some delicate

A School Called Earth

planning is now required to ensure that this other person is matched with another appropriate soul instead of you, and you do not meet and fall in love for the second time. Primary guides have a hard and frustrating time at best.

Your guide is constantly with you. They protect and guide you as much as they can, but we often choose to ignore them. You all have a third voice inside your head. It's the voice that warns you of danger, sometimes we call it our gut feeling. Learn to trust that voice, it is their form of communication.

Don't get frustrated because you cannot see your guides or angels. If you could, there would be no need to come to earth to learn the lessons you are destined to learn. Those of you who sometimes catch a glimpse of your guides or angels need to look for the specific message that they are trying to tell you. Often they do so when you are down and in need of hope. Sometimes they are trying to re-awaken your soul or confirm what you are feeling or thinking. Talk to your guides, but remember to also listen to what they are trying to tell you. Create your own language and ask for specific signs. Don't be ridiculous in your request. Don't ask to see an elephant as confirmation that your boyfriend loves you, especially if you are on the twentieth floor of an office block in the middle of a large city. Don't get despondent if the only elephant you see is on a postage stamp and you were expecting to see a real live one. The elephant on the stamp is the confirmation of your question from your guide. Be fair, they are not the Creator and do not have the power to manifest elephants on the twentieth floor of an office block. After all, it would not be very kind to the elephant unless his name was Dumbo and he could fly! Be specific, but reasonable with your request, and be careful of what you wish for, you may just get it and it may not be good for your soul's progress. If you don't progress with the lessons you have been given in this lifetime, you

A School Called Earth

will have to repeat them in the next. You can't pass grade eleven if you fail three subjects. If they do allow you to grade twelve the following year it will be on the condition that you also redo the subjects you failed in grade nine. Imagine how tough that will be. Those of you that think who your lives are tough now, should remember this!

Secondary guides
Secondary guides also form part of a sacred contract. They, however, only come into our lives from time to time and when we need very specific guidance such as healing, inspiration (in-the-spirit) or wisdom to make difficult decisions. Sometimes our passed loved ones will act as secondary guides as they have spent time with us on this earth and, therefore, understand the nature of our earthly energies and have better results at guiding us. We are familiar with their voices and energy and they will guide us in a way that they did when they lived as loved ones on this Earth.

Passed loved ones only take on the form of guides when they have achieved the right level on the other side. You won't find a nursery school child teaching a chartered accountant maths, will you? Similarly, souls on the other side can only guide you if they themselves have learnt the lesson and have reached the necessary level of soul progress. So, if your parents have passed and they were young souls, and you are an old soul, chances are they will not come visit you with an abundance of guidance. Rather they will visit you with an abundance of unconditional love.

Master guides
Master guides, guide our primary and secondary guides. These are highly advanced old souls that have long stopped incarnating. They are souls that choose or are chosen for the role of master guides, as there

are many other roles we can take on, back home. Master guides are almost pitch black in colour, indicating their closeness to the Creator. They are the most loving and kind beings I have ever met. That is all I can tell you about these blessed beings that constantly look out for us and provide us with wisdom so we too can grow, learn and eventually be as close to the Creator as they are.

Everything you learn, you learn in the now. Stop worrying about the future. It will be your present soon enough.

Do we know our Guides?
We have all, somewhere in our previous lives, been in close contact with our primary guides. Our secondary guides are often part of our soul group or cluster and, therefore, have often been a part of our current lives in the roles of family members and friends. Once we return home we will instantly recognise them and remember their names. We never forget anything back home because we are all interconnected and therefore nothing is ever forgotten.

Spirits and ghosts
I am often asked what a spirit is and what a ghost is. Is there a difference? The answer is quite simple. A spirit is a being which crosses back, from the other side (home), without a body and for a very specific reason. They may come to help or warn us against impending danger. Or they may just come over to give us love and kindness when we are down or depressed. Anyone can see a spirit, but only if the spirit wants you to.

A ghost, on the other hand, is a spirit that has not crossed over, and has decided to stay on earth. Every soul has free will and, therefore, if you choose not to go, the other side will not force you. However, when the end

A School Called Earth

comes they will be taken back whether they want to or not. Ghosts need energy to manifest or be seen by humans. They feed off our energy and especially our fear. They cannot, however, harm us in any way. Mostly the harm done to us is our own imagination getting the better of us and the result of the anxiety of fear we experience from our imaginations getting the better of us.

In the beginning there was only One.
In the end it shall be the same.

Fig 3: Ghost energy

What is an angel?
Much has been written about angels. Much of it, I am afraid, is incorrect and much of it made up but, regardless of the author, faith or religion, I have yet to find any negative word written about these most holy of God's creation.

A School Called Earth

Angels are not simple winged creatures with halos. They are, in fact, the highest realm of God's creation and the closest beings to our Creators. Like souls, angels are part of God's creation. Angels, too, are Light Energy, but unlike souls that incarnate on this earth or any other planet, angels are of the highest order of spiritual advancement and, therefore, they are the Creator's "right-hand-man" to simplify it hugely.

Some angels have, in their past, been human and, therefore, it is correct to believe that we, too, can become angels. There are earth angels all around us and most of them are not aware that they are angels. I will cover this phenomenon later. However, not all of us want to be angels. If you are one of those souls who cannot help yourself in helping others then you may be one of the souls that would enjoy the role of an angel. However, being an angel is a lot tougher than being a soul in a human body and so only the very bravest and tenacious souls choose this path.

Only highly evolved souls that have graduated beyond the stage of the Council of Elders, go on to become angels. Most highly evolved souls prefer roles as discussed in Chapter 3 under soul roles.

There are, however, certain angel types that have never incarnated as humans or any other species on any other planets. These angels are God's first creation and of the holiest order in God's creation. Their role is working with the Creator and guiding the secondary realms of the angel order. The philosopher and Catholic theologian, Thomas Aquinas (1225 –1274) wrote what are considered to be the most acclaimed angel writings called the *Summa Theologiae*. These teachings focus on the three angel realms, and try to explain why angels exist and what they exist for.

A School Called Earth

I am not privileged to see all these angelic realms and Uriall can only relay what he experiences to me. My angel experiences are fairly limited to the two lower angelic realms. My experience of angels is the closest experience to feeling the true essence of our Creator. Angels represent ultimate truth and unconditional love. Love is their only faith and they all exist to serve the Creator via helping the creation and serving its subjects – the souls. Angels serve us because they love all of God's creation, and this means us. They should, however, not replace God because, ultimately, we all exist to serve our Creator, whether we are angel or soul.

Fig 4: Prince angels as they appear to me

Fig 5: Archangels as they appear to me

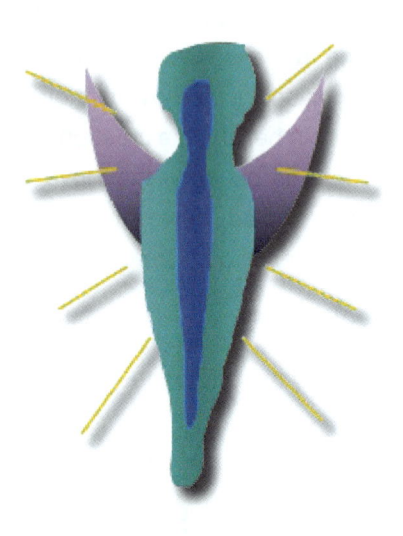

*You may not see your heart beating,
or your blood moving through your veins.
But be certain of this:
you would not be here
if your heart and blood
decided to quit.*

So it is with your Guides and Angels.

A School Called Earth

Fig 6: Guiding angels as they apear to me

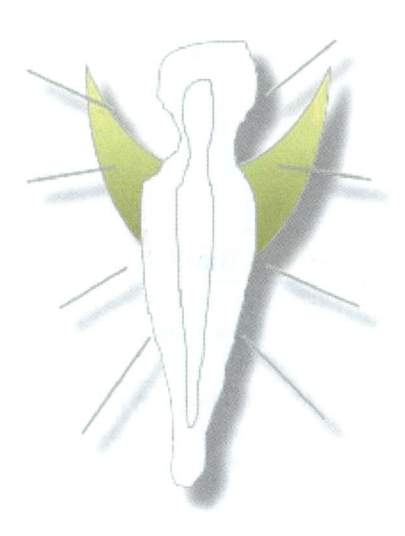

Do we all have angels at our side?
We all have secondary guides, master guides and, when the occasion calls for it, the souls of our passed loved ones that are in our soul group at our side. Behind all of these beings, will be the group of angels assigned to help and guide us on our journey on earth. These angels not only guide and protect us, but also help our guides and soul family. Most (we will have anywhere from three to twenty angels) of these angels belong to the third realm of the angel order. This order of angels, are called the celestial messengers. They, in turn, have angels of the second angelic realm helping and guiding them. The second realm is known as the teachers. The second angelic realm, in turn, has the first angelic realm assisting and guiding them, known as the holy ones.

Angel types and their roles
There are many different types of angels. Both, the angel lady, Jacky

A School Called Earth

Newcomb and my favourite teacher, Silvia Browne, have grouped them into nine different orders belonging to three different realms. Whatever you may experience or see, the importance is to give them love and, in turn, thank them for their unconditional love for us and constant guidance and protection.

Table 1. Order of the Angels

1st Order Of Angels	Role – The Holy Ones
1. Seraphim	Closest to the Creator and a part of the creative team that builds the Universe. They are the most powerful of the Angels
2. Cherubim	Work with the energy of the creation. They help with creation on planets and help with the creation of the elements that constitute life forms.
3. Thrones	They assist the council of Elders and help the planning of life paths and our destiny
2nd Order Of Angels	**Role - Teachers**
4. Dominions	They Guide the Guiding Angels who protect and Guide us.
5. Virtues	They protect the planets that Souls inhabit and control the elements of nature.
6. Powers and Carrions	They assist Souls with the crossing over process. Carrions remove negative and disruptive energies from our universe.
3rd Order Of Angels	**Role – Celestial Messengers**
7. Principles	They look after mankind and help with destiny.
8. Archangels	They are the messengers for the Creator and they are the defenders of the truth. They teach through dreams and inspiration.
9. Guiding Angels	They look over us and help protect and guide us, and our Guides.

A School Called Earth

Table 2. What Angels appear like to me.

1st Order Of Angels	Appearance
1. Seraphim	Holy prayer and joyous singing surround these magnificent beings. They emanate a bright translucent rainbow of light that heals and uplifts anything they touch.
2. Cherubim	The colour of the night lit with million stars. They create awe-inspiring energy wherever they go.
3. Thrones	They are bright white and are surrounded by energy that makes them look like they wear purple monk-like capes.
2nd Order Of Angels	**Appearance**
4. Dominions	Dark red/purple. Very solemn looking with dominating presence. They tower over cities like huge skyscrapers.
5. Virtues	Silver beings with blue wing-like energy
6. Powers and Carrions	They radiate like emeralds and tourmalines. They appear like fairies and young children.
3rd Order Of Angels	**Appearance**
7. Principles	Golden yellow with rays of energy that resemble the sun. They light up entire rooms and halls when they enter.
8. Archangels	Blue & Aquamarine with dark wing-like energies that protect us.
9. Guiding Angels	White – almost transparent. You always wonder if it was your imagination or the light playing with your imagination when you see one of these holy beings.

Earth Angels

Earth angels are advanced souls that are training to become guiding angels or master guides. These souls have stopped incarnating as humans for many hundreds of years and are only re-incarnating as they start practicing for their future roles as guiding angels or master guides. As previously stated, not all souls would like to come back to aid

A School Called Earth

other souls as guides or, even more daunting as angels. We as souls all have the grace of tapping into the greater collective conscious and the Creator's knowledge. The task of playing in this superficial world is tough enough for humans. Just imagine what a master guide or guiding angel would have to endure, knowing what they know of the other side where it is peaceful and incredibly loving.

Not all souls are alike. So, too, are angels and master guides different and, therefore, interested in different tasks. Doreen Virtue has written some revealing truths about these magnificent beings in her book *Earth Angels* (2002, Hay House). Uriall has also helped me summarise these wonderful brave beings into five extraordinary groups of loving earth angels, which I have labelled: Healers, Nurturers, Interplanetary travellers, Wise ones, Visitors. Each of these earth angel types has a very different appearance, but they all have a similarity within each group (except for the visitors). They also have their own area of expertise and each group is focused on a very specialised task. The following table explains their roles and area of focus as I have experienced.

Earth Angel Group	Roles and Appearance
The Healers	These people are the pretty Angels of the world. They are known for their kind eyes and soft sincere voices. They look like human versions of Cherub Angels you see in traditional Christian artwork. They often struggle with their bodies in terms of weight and fitness. (Especially in this world where so much emphasis is placed on looks). They have the most amazing ability to heal you or calm a room without even saying a word. They often work as spiritual healers, medical assistants, paramedics and traditional healers.

A School Called Earth

Nurturers	Often called the Earth-children of this planet. They had the perfect weapon of disguise in the hippy 1970's, but stand out a bit in the fast-paced 2k world. Nurturers are focussed on healing and protecting the world and all natural creation. You'll find that these people don't place any value on worldly possessions and would rather be outdoors in the mountains than anywhere near a city. These are the animal rescue workers or save-the-forest humans that live for a cause. They are prone to addictions of the modern world and so do better by staying away from its temptations. You will not lead these beings astray with worldly treasure.

Earth Angel Group	Roles and Appearance
Interplanetary travellers	These are the Indigo children of the modern world. These beings have probably never been to Earth before and therefore have no understanding of its processes and have very little purpose within its confines. They bring with them extraordinary talents and are here for a very specific reason involving change of human behaviour and exponential human growth. They have amazing energy and you often find them in healing professions where they use Reiki, Shiatsu or palmistry for guiding and healing Souls. These beings struggle with the management of their bodies. They find climbing stairs or driving cars a hugely difficult task, purely because they have never had to do it. Fashion also plays no role in their lives.
Wise Ones	These Earth Angels are training to become Archangels or Master Guides. These beings were the wizards, witches and sorcerers of old. Many still have past life memory and these amazing beings have the ability to heal via touch or prayer. They often become psychics or psychic mediums and spend their lives teaching humans in many different manners. They are bound to the truth of the Creator and are the spiritual messengers and hope bringers to the world.

A School Called Earth

Visitors	The new modern term for these advanced beings is a Walk-In. These Angels enter into a sacred contract with a soul that is about to commit imminent suicide and they enter the body at an opportunity created via divine intervention. The behaviour of the person changes almost overnight, and you will find that these people will not recognise places, names and will even forget what they do for a living. They will immediately change jobs and their lifestyles will become dedicated to helping humans in one way or another.

The devil, satan, fallen angels and demons

Let me start by stating the fact – there is no devil or satan and there are no demons. The worst evil you will ever meet is the flesh – man – human. At the beginning of creation the Creator looked inward and created companions to exercise thought and consideration for all that was. These magnificent beings are called the seraphim, cherubim and the thrones. These angels kept the Creator company, and were given the power to create planets and life forms. The angels, with the help of the Creator created the planets, stars and the solar systems that make up our universe. Their creation brought the Creator knowledge and experience in all that was within and so the Creator grew in love and understanding. At this stage in creation the experimentation grew to creating various life forms in all the various habitable planets of the universe and so animals were born. Many attempts were made until the animals began evolving, as we know today, from history. Then souls were created as the angels grew in knowledge of all that was. These souls began to entangle with all known matter and soon found this entanglement to be their downfall. (Perhaps this is where the story of fallen angels comes from). The Creator allowed all this as He created everything and thus knows everything. However, because of free will He allowed the continuation of this event until the separation between Creator and soul grew that the Creator had to intervene in love and grace.

A School Called Earth

Evolution, in the meantime, reached a stage where certain species of anthropoid ape evolved to such an extent that it was capable of learning and growing. This happened simultaneously in all the planets similar to earth where life forms were created. Mankind (homo sapiens, sapien) is an experiment in thought-form whereby souls can experiment with soul evolution.

The Creator, being all loving, then created a vehicle for souls to travel into the earth experiment, and we know this vehicle with a separate identity and individuality as spirit. Spirit was allowed to inhabit the species we know as primitive man in order to help these beings evolve to a level of intellect that would allow for a variety of lessons that help us reach enlightenment. Through the various lessons we learn within the bodies of this species (man), we can exercise the lessons we learn in theory in the spirit world, and as our souls evolve, we will once again be able to become pure, lose the need for personal identity and grow back and be absorbed into the Creator's love and energy. This cycle of soul evolution is what we call incarnation and it takes a soul many lifetimes on planets such as earth to reach a stage of enlightenment in order to be absorbed back into the all loving energy of the Creator.

The Creator created magnificent helping angels known as the dominions and the virtues to assist us. As man evolved, so many souls turned away from the Truth-of-the-Creator and so the powers and the carrion angels were created so that man could find the way back to the spirit world with ease.

Man needs help and guidance on a daily basis. The Creator thus gave us the magnificent guiding angels as our daily protectors and messengers back to the spirit world. The archangels brought back the truth of the Creator to the earth and helped the advanced souls with enlightenment.

A School Called Earth

The archangels furiously protected the Word of the Creator and can be found throughout history in magnificent books such as the Bible and the Kabala. Principalities angels help these highly advanced beings with planning their angelic duties so that they can grow in the love of the Creator and eventually advance their love of the Creator.

I have obviously simplified the whole creation, but the important factor here is that nowhere is there a devil that will burn your soul in eternal hellfire. The Creator loves us all. Every single one of us will eventually make our way back to Him to share in His Glory. Those that choose the way of negativity (call it evil if you like) will, eventually, lose their energy on Judgement Day, and be absorbed back into the circle of time, without having reached their goal of the Creator's enlightenment.

The souls that do not reach enlightenment when the cycle we are in, comes to an end (end of our world as we know it), will have to start the cycle all over again. A new beginning, much like a new Adam and Eve. Who wants to do it all over again?

It is only man that is evil and negative. Man rules by fear, discrimination and hatred. Man's power comes from fear and it is this fear that holds us back. We live "of the world" as opposed to "in it". We hold dear everything we can see and hold and we forget to experience the soul in the spirit so that we can grow in love for one another and our Creator. So, we choose the flesh and all that is material instead of love and all that is of soul and of the almighty Creator. We then blame a fictional character (devil or satan) for our own weakness and give it a name called sin. We blame the devil or satan for all that is bad when, in fact, we are weak and have no love. If we do love it has a condition applied to it, and this is not what the Creator and the angels have taught us. We need to learn to love the way the Creator loves us. It starts by loving ourselves so much that we

A School Called Earth

strive to become perfect souls that will go back to the Creator. If we love unconditionally, we would love everyone, of all colour, creed and race. There would be no fear, hatred, war, discrimination, crime or pain. We would, once again, recognise that we are God because the Creator, our God created us all from His own energy and therefore we are a part of Him – therefore we, too, are God the Creator. The Creator loves us all so much that He has sent many messengers to earth to show us the way to the Light (Enlightenment). These messengers, prophets are known by the names of Buddha, Jesus, Sai Baba etc. All of their lives on this earth have been filled with love, compassion and kindness for their fellow man. None have preached hatred or fear. None have tried to be powerful humans with wealth and worldly possessions. All of them love unconditionally and speak of the same love of the same Creator. None of them spend much time dwelling on the devil.

Lucifer

No angel has ever fallen from Heaven or from the Creator's grace. What you have been told is an abomination of the word of our all-loving Creator. Deal with it. Here comes the truth. There is proof on this earth, yet we choose to ignore the records that exist in libraries around the world, choosing rather to follow the dogma which binds us into a life of eternal fear and suffering. Please do yourself a favour, and read some of Zecharia Sitchin's work. This remarkable million-copy, best-selling author and researcher has spent over fifty years studying and deciphering the Sumerian tablets, which detail the origins of mankind, going back 450 000 years. Locally, there is a brilliant author by the name of Michael Tellinger who has written a fabulous book called *Slave Species of god*. I highly recommend that you read it.

Okay, so you want a shortened version and you want it now! Here is what Uriall has to say about where the lie of the fallen angels comes

A School Called Earth

from. Luciff (means light), Ur (means earth) thus lower-light. Lucifer is the original sin known to man, but not one created by the angels that live in the spirit world. The sin comes from a being that fell out of grace of his father who, at his time on this earth, convinced mankind that he was god when, in actual fact, he was no more advanced than we were by the year 2000.

Uriall confirms that the Sumerian tablets are fairly accurate.

Approximately 450 000 years ago astronauts from a highly advanced civilisation called the Anunnaki arrived on Earth from a distant planet in our solar system called Nibiru. They are facing extinction as their "Ozone" layer is eroding and they are in desperate need of gold which, when refined, can be used to protect their planet's atmosphere. They are lead by an overthrown leader called Alalu. Earth's climate is still very harsh, with continent shifts and volcanic activity taking place. It is not a wonderful place to live, but they need the gold, which lies in abundance on the earth.

The planet Nibiru circumnavigates the Sun once in 3600 years, so the Anunnaki live a long time, compared to human years.

Approximately 445 000 years ago, Enki, son of the Anunnaki King Anu, arrives on earth for the purpose of establishing a mining station called Eridu. Eridu is situated near the Persian Gulf, where the waters are full of easily obtainable gold. The mass mining begins. The Anunnaki is a highly advanced race that has the ability to travel in space and, therefore, mining and extracting gold is not impossible for them. Later, Enki's half-sister Ninharsag arrives with more Anunnaki. She is the head medical officer for the Anunnaki on earth.

A School Called Earth

Then, approximately 416 000 years ago, as gold runs short in the Persian Gulf, king Anu arrives on Earth, bringing with him the next heir to the throne Enlil. Enki is sent to southern Africa where more gold has been found, and Enlil stays in Eridu. Anu then returns to Nibiru, but not before he is challenged for the throne, by Alalu's grandson, Kumarbi. Kumarbi is part of a group of astronauts that stay in a space station above the earth. In this space station they collect the gold-ore mined on earth and from this space station they load up space ships, and send them back to Nibiru. The astronauts are known as Igigi (Those in the heavens that see everything).

16 000 years later, there are seven functional Anunnaki mining settlements around the Earth, all shipping the gold ore to Eridu, which is then sent back to Nibiru. The Igigi, lead by Kumarbi, grow restless and challenge Enlil for reign over the earth. They lose the war known as the War of the Olden Gods.

Much later, approximately 300 000 years ago, the Anunnaki on Earth no longer want to mine gold, so Enki and Ninharsag create a primitive worker by genetically enhancing the DNA of apewoman. This new breed, known as homo-sapiens takes over the mining work in Africa (Cradle of Mankind). Enlil, against Enki's wishes, takes some of these primitive workers back to his home base near Mesopotamia, known as Edin. Homo sapiens do what they do best and start to multiply. The experienced mineworkers are taken to various parts of the globe, which we now know as North and South America, Japan, India and Australia.

Approximately 100 000 years ago, to Enlil's disgust, the Anunnaki, procreate with homo sapiens (Biblical writings call it the Nefilim marrying the daughters of man). 75 000 years ago an Ice Age began, and only Cro-Magnon man survived. Enki and Ninharsag give the offspring of

A School Called Earth

homo sapiens and their Anunnaki masters an elevated status over the rest of the primitive workers. Enlil is enraged by these actions where the Anunnaki play the role of god. He plans to destroy mankind.

By 11, 000 BC, Nibiru is close to passing near earth and Enlil realises that this will have a catastrophic effect on the earth. Tidal waves are expected, and Enlil sees this as an opportunity to end mankind. He makes the Anunnaki swear to keep the imminent catastrophe a secret from mankind, but Enki loves his Nefilim creation and plans to save his son Ziusudra (Noah). He teaches Ziusudra how to build a submersible ship and all the Anunnaki leave to watch the total destruction from their orbiting spacecraft.

Ziusudra lives through the flood and Enlil grants the remnants of mankind the ability to grow crops and agriculture begins. Enki teaches them how to domesticate animals, and the rest is biblical history. What we don't know is that Enki's firstborn son Ra/Marduk ruled over Egypt as a god. The pyramids are built as homing beacons for spaceships. The Anunnaki are a bunch of greedy, power-hungry characters and there is seldom peace as they struggle for power over the earth. Enki and Enlil are constantly at each other's throats and finally Ninharsag intervenes and establishes peace between the two brothers. By 3800 BC, urban civilization is flourishing in Sumer and the Sumerians are taught the art of writing. They are taught the history of the Anunnaki, which they capture on clay tablets, found in museums all over the world today.

In 3760 BC mankind is given its first kingship, yet the Anunnaki maintain supreme control over the earth and all its gold mining operations. By 2023 BC, the Anunnaki have taken all the gold they need and it is time to leave. They destroy Sumer with a wind that carries radioactive/chemical cloud.

A School Called Earth

The Anunnaki and Nefilim appeared as gods to man, and their soldiers, as angels that could fly. They seemed immortal, as one year to them is 3600 to us. They abused their power, and what they left us with was a legacy and desire for gold, war, power and slavery. We still have this obsession for gold and power today. Have you ever wondered how primitive man could extract gold from stone 4000 years ago, but only developed the wheel some 2500 years ago?

Their story has been incorrectly passed on in our scriptures, where we often confuse God with the Anunnaki self-proclaimed gods, and spiritual angels with Anunnaki astronauts, the Igigi. The god often written about in the ancient scriptures is not our Creator of unconditional love, and the warrior-like angels that always seemed to appear just before or just after a huge catastrophe, are not our loving guiding angels. These gods raped the earth of all that was good, and used man as labour, mining the earth of all its gold and other precious minerals. Many of their descendants still live on this earth, whether they know it or not. The Anunnaki have souls too. But some of those souls sinned by their actions on this earth. They are the original sinners, the so-called "angels" that fell from the sky (Heaven) and sinned against our Creator.

I am not blaspheming against the scriptures, but I am pointing out that behind many of the Old-Testament scriptures, are stories that have been told incorrectly, or told by the gods, who wanted man to see them as God. These beings have confused mankind for approximately 300 000 years, making mankind believe that they were, in fact, the only gods. Unfortunately the true accounts of angels and the Creator have been intertwined with these lies, making it incredibly difficult to decipher truth from instructed lies by the Anunnaki gods. However, you all have a soul and several angels and guides with you. Use your intuition to unravel the truth. When the truth passes through your soul, you will feel it and

A School Called Earth

accept it, as it becomes a part of your make-up. When it's a lie, your mind will chew on it uncomfortably, and should you accept the lie as your truth, you will find yourself becoming very angry with anyone who should challenge your new belief. You see, the truth is just that: the truth, so it matters not whether anyone believes or agrees with you because your senses will tell you that the truth will always be just that. But a lie that gets cast in concrete feels very vulnerable and gets very defensive when challenged, because it knows it has very little substance to defend its stance and stands a very real possibility of becoming extinct.

So, to conclude this chapter, I want you to know that neither I nor any of my regression research clients have ever seen lucifer or satan or any fallen angel. There is no evil devil, satan or lucifer, other than the one created by your own imagination and the fact that you believe the lie gives substance to it. You have been lied to and you were lead to believe that the lie came from our Creator, when, in fact, it came from the evil Anunnaki gods. "Lucifer" is evil, because lucifer is a lie told to mankind, and so the lie is the original sin. But here is no evil angel waiting in hell to burn you in eternal damnation, if you should sin. The closest you will ever get to that illusion, is when you have a terrible time in this school I call Earth.

I once knew a man with hatred in his heart for his fellow man.
Hatred gave him the fuel to condemn and criticise.

I found out later that he died of a heart attack.

Our bodies are designed for love.
Feed it hatred and it will surely kill you.

CHAPTER 6
Why Earth is Such A Tough School

A Tough school for fast learners
Welcome fellow souls (some of you are even alien) to the planet earth! Why earth? Well, it's probably the most complex school planet of them all. The Creator has given us many planets where we as souls can go to learn many wonderful lessons. I am not going to spend too much time in this area in this book, but there are many planets, either more advanced or less advanced, where the soul has the opportunity to learn lessons varying from primitive existence to highly advanced and highly spiritual. Some planets have beings, just like humans, yet they are technologically much more advanced. Planets like Nibiru, where scientific evolvement does not necessarily mean spiritual advancement. Earth is a rather mediocre planet with average advancement of the species; yet the lessons we learn here are combinations of what we can learn in several other planets. For this reasons, many brave souls choose earth where the lessons are tough but our soul advancement is rapidly accelerated. Souls on the other side consider souls that incarnate on earth to be really brave, courageous and just a little bit looney.

School is a place where people go to learn, right? So how do we benefit from this school called earth, and how can we ensure that we don't get bashed by the school bullies or treated like dirt by the pretty girl who is loved by everyone – even though she is the shallowest, stupidest most self-absorbed guppy in the fish bowl? The answer is simple, and it involves free will. If your soul wants to learn a lesson the lesson will happen, regardless of how you, the human being, feel about it.

A School Called Earth

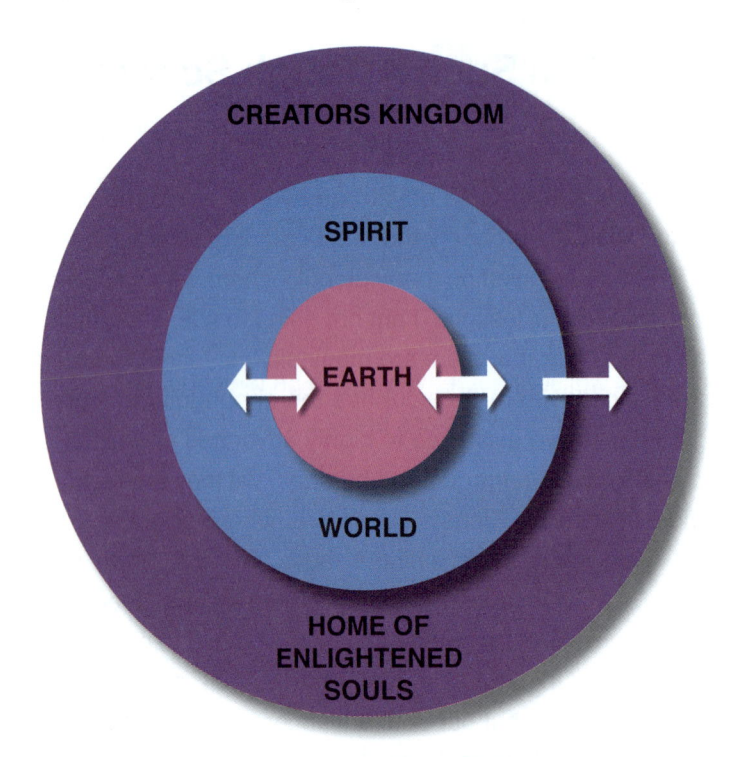

The Earth, Other Side and the Kingdom of Heaven

```
CREATORS KINGDOM
    SPIRIT
    EARTH
    WORLD
HOME OF
ENLIGHTENED
SOULS
```

As Souls in the incarnation process, we move between the earth plane and the spirit world. Once we have achieved enlightenment, we progress to the Creator's Kingdom and, once again, become one with Him. In the spirit world our souls live inside our spirit vessel. In the spirit world we often take on the form we most enjoyed back on the earth plane. The spirit world is filled with love and we are part of the universal mind. We know everything, but we have not experienced everything. Knowing something does not mean understanding it and so we travel to schools like earth so we can practise the lessons. The spirit world is not our final destination, but a place where we go to rest, learn, love and be loved unconditionally. However, souls are by nature curious and impatient.

A School Called Earth

They want to exercise their free will to experience the lessons that other souls around them already understand. The Creator, like a loving parent, does not want us to experience suffering, but we insist on the challenges that incarnating into human beings have for us. And so, like a loving, yet concerned parent, the Creator agrees to send us off to school, knowing that we will encounter difficulties and bullies. He knows that some of the experiences will leave us scarred, but the Creator knows that, once we go back home, His loving parental embrace will make it all better, till the next practise run. As we evolve as students, we become braver, until we eventually look forward to going to school. Whilst at school, we want to go home, and whilst at home we want to go to school, even if it's only to play with our friends during class breaks. We are never satisfied.

After many years of going to school, we start to understand how school is a place where we can equip ourselves with knowledge that will help us become better adults in the future. Not that you learn all the lessons at school, but we know that the curriculum has been designed by scholars far brighter than us, and so we go back until we have learnt all that school can teach us.

Once we have graduated from school, some of us go back home, some of us become parents and others become teachers. Some go on and further their studies and then become the teachers who teach the teachers. Ultimately, we retire and live the rest of our days quietly, reflecting on the lessons and waiting for a final trip home.

Introduction to free will
Before you start blaming God or anyone else including the non-existent devil, I would like to remind you of free will – and no, I'm not talking about the killer whale movie! We have all been given free will and this is the root of most our evil-doings. This school has some really incredible

A School Called Earth

lessons we as souls can learn. Some of the lessons are fantastic, while others are really tough. For every positive there always is a negative. Here are some of the tough ones:

- Cruelty
- Racism
- Poverty
- Pain and suffering
- Abuse
- Discrimination
- Rejection
- Cruel people
- Child abuse
- Fear
- Suffering
- Jealousy
- Greed

There are too many to mention and you don't need reminding as you come across them daily. However, some of these lessons are as wonderful as:

- Love
- Fun
- Receiving
- Popularity

And then some are really beautiful and rare, such as

- **Wisdom**
- **Bravery**
- **Enlightenment**

The purpose of coming to earth is to understand the reason behind the lessons. So before you want to blame the Creator, man or the world, you

A School Called Earth

need to seek the wisdom of interpretation of your lessons and you need to ask the Creator, the angels and your guides for the bravery to overcome your weaknesses and the wisdom to understand your purpose. When you are able to convert your lesson into spiritual knowledge, the Creator grows and your soul reaches a step closer to Him. As a soul you are rewarded in love when you are able to conquer over adversity (racism, ignorance, pain, sexism, discrimination or just plain stupidity). You do so by sending love to the person who has done you wrong and, in doing so, the Creator bestows love unconditionally upon you.

But before you write an exam or tackle a task, you need to plan. So, too, you need to plan your life to obtain spiritual growth and enlightenment. Here is a diagram that could perhaps help you with your planning for spiritual development. Remember, without a plan, you will constantly feel lost, as if something is missing in your life. Also, important to remember is that having a plan for spiritual growth does not mean living in the future, stressing about the outcome. Live in the now, but plan your now in the future.

A School Called Earth

Diagram of life planning

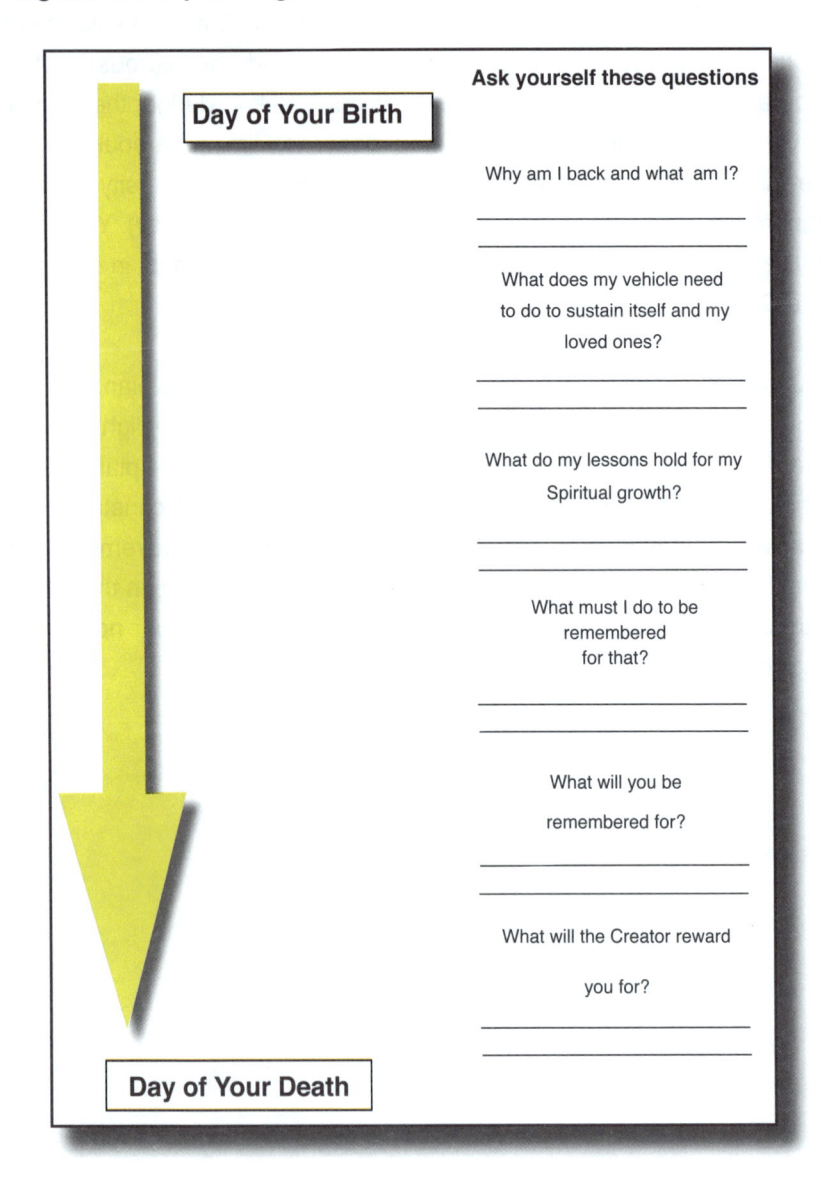

Day of Your Birth

↓

Day of Your Death

Ask yourself these questions

Why am I back and what am I?
_____
_____

What does my vehicle need to do to sustain itself and my loved ones?
_____
_____

What do my lessons hold for my Spiritual growth?
_____
_____

What must I do to be remembered for that?
_____
_____

What will you be remembered for?
_____
_____

What will the Creator reward you for?
_____
_____

Chapter 7
Case Studies – the proof you have been waiting for

Introduction to hypnotherapy and regression

I run a hypnotherapy consulting practice and mostly focus on work as a trauma counsellor and regressional hypnotherapist. I have dedicated my life to the Creator and His will is that I protect the Truth of the Creator by teaching the Word to my fellow man. The reason for this is that we are running out of time on this earth and we still have much to learn before we can become one with the Creator. I have previously explained the Creation and the circle of time we are in. This planet of ours has little time left. Probably less than 100 years, and yet there are millions of souls that have not progressed past their young soul stage. Life is precious and each one holds the lessons we require to grow spiritually until we reach enlightenment. Yet the world we live in is spiralling further away from the truth, entangled in a web of deceit. We focus on worldly wealth and power, and we have forgotten why we are here and most importantly, we have forgotten to love our Creator in the way that he planned for us.

As I have previously said, in this life I have always been the holy spirit's messenger. I have always had visions and always been claircognisant. I was born this way. However, I did not always talk about it as it scared people and I was not aware of my purpose in this life. It is only once I had become a hypnotherapist and started doing regressional hypnotherapy that I truly believed that what the Creator had bestowed upon me is my gift. As my clients spoke under hypnotic regression of the things I thought only I could see, I came to understand that my gift of sight was not for me alone, but to be shared with mankind. I am on earth to speak of the truth of our Creator and, as I do so, I hopefully awaken your soul to follow its own chosen path back home.

Hypnotherapy has been around for as long as man has exercised his mind over matter. The hypnotherapist has no power over you. 95% of what you have heard is myth. Stage hypnotists have ruined a beautiful way in which we as souls can connect with our higher self and learn the purpose of our incarnation. Together, with the doctrine of fear-based religions, we have become sceptics of everything we cannot see. We would rather criticise than explore. We are nothing short of cowards, afraid of the dark. The earth was once believed to be flat. Anyone that dared profess any different theory was put to death. Nowadays, we are not put to death for speaking of the unknown, but the rejection of psychics as frauds bears a resemblance.

Past life regression
In hypnosis, the focus is to take the mind from the conscious state known as the beta state, to a state of sub-consciousness called the alpha state. If the mind slows down further it enters into a deeper super-consciousness state, known as the theta state. This is the state just before we fall into deep sleep.

Our soul resides in the super-conscious mind state. Our soul mind has knowledge of the entire universe, of all that exists on the other side and all the memories of past lives. Our soul drives our mind and our consciousness. Therefore our soul leaves us messages in our sub-conscious mind when it wants to communicate with our consciousness. Think of the sub-consciousness as a post-box, where our spiritual messages are left for our conscious minds to collect. This is why inspiration normally reaches us when we are relaxed and daydreaming (When we daydream, we are mostly in a sub-conscious state). When we meditate, we quiet our minds and tap into, firstly, the sub-conscious mind and then, with practise, the super-conscious mind. By this process, we tap into our soul mind, where all our past memories reside. In hypnosis the same is

A School Called Earth

achieved by collaboration between hypnotist, client and the client's soul. In regression, once we reach the super-conscious mind, the hypnotist communicates directly with the soul of the client, so that messages of life purpose and unfinished past life challenges can be brought back into the client's conscious mind. This is how we gain insight into our purpose here in our present incarnation.

In past-life regression, clients get to experience several of their past lives and, through these experiences, get to better understand their nature, their current karmic lessons and why they chose the lives they now live. After a regression session all my clients feel an inner peace they have never felt before. Past-life experiences give them a sense of deeper understanding of why they have to experience some of the tough lessons on this earth. I have yet to meet a client that has shown any regret from a regression session.

Figure x: The process of tapping into the past life memories of the soul through hypnosis

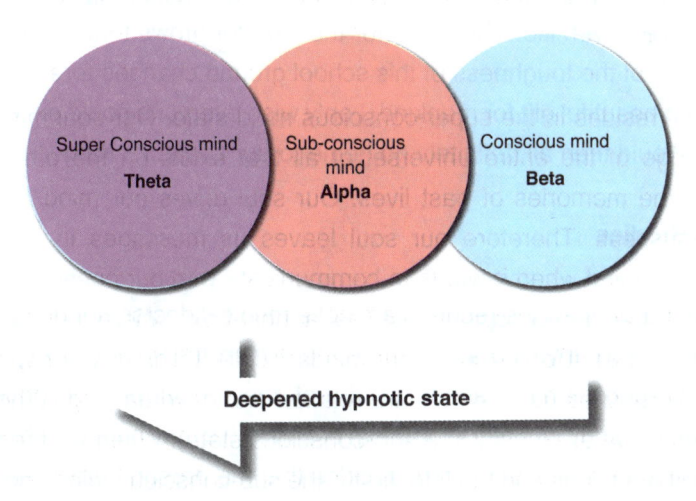

Super Conscious mind — Theta

Sub-conscious mind — Alpha

Conscious mind — Beta

Deepened hypnotic state

Life between-life regressions (LBLR)
Past-life regressions are fairly well known amongst hypnotherapy circles.

A School Called Earth

Michael Newton made LBLR known to the world in the book *Journey/Destiny of Souls*. Since then, I have been practising LBLR and it is this wonderful discovery that has made me comfortable talking about what I can see. 100% of my clients in LBLR speak about the spirit world, the angels, guides and the Creator in exactly the same way and, if this is not enough proof, then nothing will ever be.

You may argue that all of my clients have read Michael Newton and, therefore, have similar answers. For this reason I always ask the client to visit my soul group and confirm the group members. This way, no one can cheat and I am glad to say that every time they meet with my soul group back home on the other side, the same souls are met with and confirmation of an accurate and true LBLR is made.

In LBLR sessions, the client is taken back to the other side. There they meet with their soul family, their guides and their angels. After such an experience my client's lives are changed forever and they start to lead a purpose-driven life. Their love for the Creator grows tenfold, and their tolerance of the toughness of this school ground changes forever. LBLR is truly a beautiful gift for mankind. I only wish everyone could experience it. We would then all definitely go home to our Creator's Kingdom.

Case Studies

Let me be clear for the record. I am not a medical doctor, nor do I profess to understand anything about medicine. When the spirit (holy spirit), or Uriall, diagnoses a disease for my client, they do so, by highlighting the area on the body where the problem occurs. This may happen whilst I am consulting or at any time spirit decides that the person I am near needs help. Spirit has, on some occasions, asked me to approach strangers in shopping malls to give them advice. It requires every bit of courage I

A School Called Earth

have on these difficult, but often inspiring occasions. The advice is not to take a certain medicine, but rather to seek certain medical advice or, in most cases, it requires that the client take some sort of corrective action for the soul to find a balance within the client's life.

In a consultation with a client, where the client often comes for a hypnotic regression, I tap into the Other Side, and either spirit or Uriall will come through with words of advice for my client. Often the client does not know what is wrong with them, or if they do know, they usually have run out of medical solutions to finding help.

It has taken me most of my life to come to accept that I have to pass on to friends, clients and strangers, the diagnosis that spirit or Uriall give me without questioning and without doubt. Never has spirit or Uriall, caused me any embarrassment or criticism from the person I have relayed the message too. It is amazing that I had never noticed this before and, thinking back, I cannot understand why I have always been so nervous. They are never wrong. Sometimes, however, I do not understand what they are saying, because I have no knowledge of the disease or condition the client has.

Now that I have embraced my gift and accepted the challenge that this life holds for me, I do find it easier to do the work that spirit and Uriall guide me towards. Thanks-be to the Creator for my courage to do the work He intended for me.

Once you equip yourself with the knowledge of the Holy Spirit.
Everything in your life becomes a matter of fact.
Taking action however, still requires practice.

A School Called Earth

Case Study 1:

A story about finding the courage, to let go of the past

Ann was different from all the children around her. As a child growing up, she had a close relationship with God, even though she never went to church or followed a religion. She always felt a presence around her. She called it her angels. Ann was always outspoken, always fiercely independent, and always different to the crowd. Ann has a beautiful face like that of a model you'd expect to see on the cover of a woman's magazine. She has a magnetic presence, and people would either be attracted to this beautiful child, or be afraid of her strong persona. Ann grew up in a tough and poor neighbourhood on the Natal South Coast and, as a teenager, she found happiness in surfing, playing on the beach or spending time with her cousins and friends. In her late teens, Ann fell in love with a good-looking surfer boy. Their love was a whirlwind romantic story, straight out of a paperback romance novel. Until she fell pregnant that is. She had a beautiful baby boy, but that was the last she saw of the father. Ann's not the kind of woman who suffers fools. She neither needs a man, nor lets a man run her life, and she soon got on to her feet. Her life, though, was not without an extra dose of disasters, her only joy being her son, Ben, who has turned into a wonderful and loving teenager - her pride and joy. Today, Ann runs a successful hair salon, but Ann was in desperate need of help, both physically and emotionally.

By the time Ann had decided to seek alternative help, her endometriosis was in an advanced state. She had given up hope and, besides being physically uncomfortable most of the time, she was struggling with weight gain, and hence low self esteem. Ann's earlier tough and troubled childhood left her feeling she was jinxed and accident-prone. She had been in several severe car accidents that left her nervous and scared

A School Called Earth

of driving. In South Africa if you don't drive, you don't go anywhere. Her world's walls seemed to be closing in, and Ann was slowly becoming paranoid and trouble seemed to follow her everywhere. Being hijacked outside her home did not make matters any easier. Ann's secrets of child abuse, both physical and emotional were surfacing in her subconscious mind, and these pent-up emotions made her aggressive and difficult to approach. She went from one failed relationship to the next. Life was no longer fun, she needed help desperately, but psychiatrists and doctors failed to find a suitable cure.

Ann woke up one morning in late October 2003, and said out loud to the Angel Michael. "Please, I need help. Please, will you send me some help! I have had enough of this suffering and I am lonely."

I had met Ann once before, and on this same day in late October, I phoned my ex-wife, Deirdre, to ask her what I should make for dinner. She was having her hair cut at Ann's hair salon and Ann was personally doing her hair. As soon as I spoke to Deirdre I sensed the familiar "quickening", that I feel when spirit comes through. Spirit does not wait for my permission to come through, nor does spirit come through when my client asks. In this case spirit felt like getting involved with Ann's healing.

Deirdre was used to my communication sessions at what seems to be the most inappropriate times, so she smiled at Ann and passed her the phone.

What happened next has changed Ann's life forever.

Luis   Hi Ann, Luis here, what do you want? (Spirit told me to ask her what she wanted so I asked).

A School Called Earth

Ann What do you mean, what do I want?

Luis You asked for help this morning did you not? Can you be more specific, what exactly is it that you want?

Ann How do you know I asked for help (sounding very sceptical and a little alarmed)?

Luis Well Ann, You asked the Angel Michael (spirit presented Itself to me in the form of a male angel and I sensed he was one of the Michaelilu) for help this morning, and he is here with me now and would like me to help you, but I don't know everything, so you need to give me some sort of direction with what you mean by "I need help and I need it now!"

Note: You may be wondering why Michael did not just tell me everything that was wrong with Ann, and what I needed to do for Ann, but I believe that this is a part of my lesson in learning to help others.

Ann That's impossible, how could you possibly know that I asked the Angel Michael for anything? (Clients always want proof, and sometimes I am tempted to give them an extra special dosage of my psychic medicine)

Luis Well ok Ann, you want a bit of proof so here it is. Hmmm, there are six clients in your salon including Deirdre; on your left there are two ladies, one blond elderly lady in a white top and one short dark haired Asian lady, who can barely speak a word of English. I think she works in the same building as you. Behind you there are three people, one lady with pitch-black hair, no, wait she works for you, a young man sitting in a chair with a lady with bright red hair, looks like she works for you too. Sorry, make those three clients and three staff members.

Ann (Silence)

Luis Hi Ann, you ok?

Ann Bloody hell, when did you say I can come and see you?

Luis How's next Friday at 4pm?

When Ann came to see me she looked nervous. It was partly because she had to drive through heavy traffic and partly because she had been to several mediums and hypnotherapists and there had been no change in her condition.

Immediately as she sat down, spirit came through. First, I introduced Ann to her past, as spirit gave me her life history as proof that I am not a fraud and to help her calm down. I asked her about certain people she knew that had passed on and explained why certain things had happened to her throughout her life. I explained the lessons in every event and explained to her the meaning behind the lessons.

We then did a spiritual regression where I desensitised the traumatic memories from her past. The next hour was spent using the power of the Holy Spirit, as we transferred healing energy to the area of the endometriosis. When Ann awoke to full consciousness, she felt calm and relaxed.

Ann returned for several more healing sessions and every time I saw her she had lost 3 to 4 kilos. Ann's life is once again balanced. She lost all the weight she wanted to and, more importantly, has found a loving partner, and their relationship has a sound foundation of love and understanding. She now constantly talks to the Angels and every now and again puts them to the test. They never cease to surprise her and sometimes they even scare her when she asks for tricks like flashing the lights in her salon. She has found inner peace and has focused her life on spiritual growth. She thanks the Creator every day.

Case Study 2:

Cathy: Diagnosed with leukaemia and pregnant – How to find the courage to persevere in the face of death.

In front of me sat a beautiful brunette with a slender build. I knew nothing about her other than that she had leukaemia. She was pale and weak from the chemotherapy. The happiest day of her life was when she found out that she was pregnant. It was also the most traumatic, because it was the day she found out she had leukaemia. The doctors suggested she terminate the pregnancy so she could undergo treatment. They warned her that if she went the full term, the baby may survive, but the childbirth would surely kill her. They also warned her that the treatment might leave the baby disabled or retarded. She opted for small doses of chemotherapy and regular blood transfusions to increase her dangerously low red blood cell level. She felt physically terrible and had lost all hope of a happy future. Furthermore, she was afraid of dying and leaving her new husband, who had lost his first wife to cancer, alone again. The weight of the world was on her shoulders and no help seemed to be on the way. Earlier that week, she had prayed to the angels for help. She believed they would cure her. Her faith was awe-inspiring.

Luis   Cathy, let me start by saying this. You are pregnant!

A School Called Earth

Cathy   Yes I know! (Clients often keep things from me to see whether I am for real).

Luis   Your baby daughter assures me that you will both be fine. You have help on its way.

Luis   Who is Paula? She has crossed over. She is now in the room with us. She says that you two are close on the other side, but on earth you did not meet. You have been together on this earth before, as sisters, she tells me. You even look alike.

Cathy   She is my husband's first wife. She died of cancer.

Luis   Yes well, she is on her way back. She is going to be your daughter in this lifetime. Together you will love Grant.

Cathy   Scary, how did you know his name?

Luis   You wrote it on the forms I gave you!

Cathy laughed so hard the tears were streaming down here face. I love to use humour as it lightens the situation and relaxes my clients.

Luis   Moving on then, Paula also says she was psychic on this earth?

Cathy   Yes, Grant's friends say so.

Luis   She feels terrible for leaving Grant, but this was a contract you three agreed to, before coming to earth. It's the only way you could all learn this lesson of grief together. You three are inseparable back at home, so you often incarnate together. You, however, decided to take on courage as an extra dose. You are a tough soul. You have taken on some seriously tough lessons.

Cathy I don't feel tough, but I guess you are right, I can be if I have to. Suppose in this case I have no choice, right?

Luis You always have choice. It's the one gift no one can take from us. Your choices may be narrowed by your circumstance, but you will still have a choice.

Luis Cathy, there is another spirit behind you. Says his name is Andre. Says he was a pilot and that you knew him. Also tells me that there is something wrong with Grant's mouth.

Cathy Andre was a friend, and yes he was a pilot.

Luis What is with the mouth problem?

Cathy Grant has just had a mouth operation to fix his jaw. Wow, now I believe you.

Luis Good, the reason he gave me some proof is so that you will believe my next statement from Andre. It is not your time to die. You need to believe this.

Cathy I don't want to die. I want to have this baby. I want to be happy with Grant. Please help.

Luis Let's get started.

A School Called Earth

The hypnotic regression came with ease. Cathy instantly regressed to a past life where she described her environment in the most amazing detail. Cathy (Carla) as she was called in that life was a young girl in 1888 with a positive demeanour. She was from a wealthy family, living in Boston, USA. Everybody loved her, especially the children in the nearby town, who surrounded her in her frequent trips to the shops. She always bought them sweets. Yet, Carla was becoming sick and the doctors could not find a cause. They suspected the rare blood disease we now call leukaemia.

Carla's family were very distraught, and all the money in the world could not save their daughter. Her sister Elizabeth (Paula in this lifetime) took the news of Carla's illness the worst, and even her new lover St John's (Grant in this lifetime) efforts to cheer her with romance and love could not take away her pain. What Elizabeth or anyone else never knew was that Carla was in love with St John and, knowing she could not have him, made her give up the will to live. Carla died a few weeks after her thirtieth birthday. Elizabeth eventually married St John and had two daughters, yet she carried her sister's loss throughout her life, mourning her death till the day she died herself. John visited both gravestones on their respective birthdays till the day he crossed over, vowing to always love the sisters in the afterlife, as he had for all his life. He still does.

In the regression I removed the past life trauma from Cathy, and helped her soul come to terms with the death. This desensitising of the past soul memory helps the soul deal with the lesson of the past life, and so the soul has no need to continue with the lesson in this current life. What happened is that as Cathy's soul became ready in this life to deal with crossing over as it had in the past life, Cathy developed leukaemia once again (It could have been any disease that would have lead to her early death). Now that Cathy's soul was healed from her early untimely crossing over, and has her past life memory has been dealt with, her new body did not need to prepare for an early crossing over. Her healing had begun. There was no reason to die, as there were new lessons to be learnt. Also it was her time to spend a happy life on earth with St John!

Once Cathy came out of the regression, she understood the reason for her leukaemia. She also understood that it was caused by her soul's past life memory, and that the disease was not destined for her new body. She recognised both Grant and Paula as members of her soul group, who reincarnate together as they grow in wisdom, through the lessons they choose for themselves. She stopped being the victim and took her power back. A few months later her baby daughter was born. Her leukaemia was in remission and she was on her way to a healthy and enlightened life. She has the most amazing faith and the strongest will I have ever met in a person. Her sense of the Creator is beautiful and humbling.

I visited Cathy and Grant at their new home and got to see the new baby Cynthia. Cynthia (Paula) recognised me immediately. Babies can't talk, but the soul can still communicate. As I waved goodbye, I heard Paula in my mind saying thank you. I am grateful that I was able to help Cathy's soul find a purpose

Case Study 3:

Barbara: Loss of a child – How to find hope and love in the face of an untimely death – bereavement

Once a month when I started my spiritual talks, I used to conduct a talk at a friend of mine's hair salon. She would invite her esoteric clients for a "crossing-over" talk where I would share my knowledge of the spirit world. At the end of each session I would tap in to the spirit world and

A School Called Earth

bring back messages of hope and love from passed loved ones and family. On this specific day back in July 2004, I met a beautiful young spirit named Paul, who came to say hello to his grieving mom.

Barbara, an attractive woman in her late thirties with a commanding presence and radiant smile, sat to my left. Behind the façade, however, was a sad mom who had not come to terms with the death of her son two years earlier. She still had many questions and was fast loosing her faith in God. What happened next, will live with me forever.

I was talking about souls and guides when a young boy (spirit) interrupted me. Normally, I ask them to wait till I have finished the topic, but Paul was having none of it and insisted on talking to me. I looked back at Uriall, who just shrugged and gave me a rather wicked "now you're in for it" smile.

Luis   Sorry to stop the talk here folks, but I have a young boy here by the name of Paul. Tells me one of you is his mom. I think it is you, I said pointing to Barbara.

For the record, I do not like to make people feel uncomfortable in my talks, but I have learnt never to hold back when the spirit world is that insistent.

Luis   Hi, Sorry for being so forward, but did you have a son called Paul? He is insisting it is you and he knows that you are sceptical and you don't believe a word I am saying but, nevertheless, he has much to say to you.

Barbara   Hi, um yes, I did have a son called Paul, he died...

Luis   Wait, don't tell me another thing. Paul will confirm everything so that when he gives you a message, you will believe.

A School Called Earth

Barbara   Ok then, go on.

Luis   Barbara, do you have a picture with you? Wait, no, do you have a picture in a frame with you? Strange that you carry the whole frame with you, but Paul insists on this story.

Barbara   No it's not strange, I do carry the picture in the frame with me.

Luis   Ok then, I feel better now, we are moving in the right direction. Paul shows me that something happened to the photo. Looks like a mark around his neck, I think it means that he broke his neck, something about a car accident.

Barbara was tearful now. Paul's information was accurate. He was an excellent communicator and his messages were clear enough for me to give the message spot on. She pulled the photo frame with the picture of Paul out of her rather large handbag and showed to me and the rest of the audience. The photo had a watermark over the area of Paul's neck. The audience went dead quiet. No one moved or uttered a single sound.

Barbara   This is my favourite photo of Paul. At about the same time of the car accident in which Paul died from a broken neck, the photo fell off the wall in our lounge, and the watermark appeared over that area almost at the same time. I have never understood why. I still have so many questions. Why is God punishing me, why did he have to take my son? Why, why?

Luis   God is not punishing you. It was Paul's soul's choice to leave this earth school. He has come back to train as your guide, but

A School Called Earth

he first wanted to spend some physical time with you so that he could understand how you think. Time in your womb and time in your family has helped him understand your human brain and your emotional side. Paul also tells me he felt no pain when he died, so stop worrying about the accident. He crossed over before the impact. It was over before the accident started. Paul is a highly advanced soul learning how to become a guide. On the other side, Paul is one of your teachers, and he has come back to teach you once again.

Barbara So does that mean he is ok?

Luis He is better than ok, he is brilliant and he is always with you, always will be. You need to believe that he loves you, and that from this day forward he is with you as your teacher. You can talk to him all day long. He will always listen. You now need to learn how to listen to him, you need to learn to pray and meditate. You need to be grateful for having such a wonderful and highly advanced soul spend so much time with you, both physically in this life as your son, and now spiritually as you guide. You will still feel sorrow for the loss of your son, but the Creator loves you and the two of you are still together. Paul is sorry that he has caused you pain, but he and you both agreed on this lesson long before you were born. It's now time to continue the love you have for each other and the Creator as you gain wisdom and enlightenment together.

I never saw or heard from Barbara again, but Paul came back one evening for a visit. He told me that his mom had, once again, regained her faith and love for the Creator. She has now embraced her lesson. Paul looked really happy. He said thanks.

Ask, but if you don't receive,
Get up
And ask again.
Or how serious is your need that
You only ask one?

Case Study 4: Rape victim – struggling with anxiety and a self-destructive attitude to relationships – finding courage in a tough school.

I met Janet, a young at heart forty-something, over the phone. She had heard about regression and was wondering if it could cure her anxiety. Janet had been raped as a teenager, and had never recovered from the trauma. She had two sons from a failed marriage, and relationships just never seemed to go right. She kept finding herself with abusive men and wanted desperately to stop the cycle of self-destruction. Her anxiety when with partners never allowed her to open up and soon she would be back to self-loathing, which in turn heightened the anxiety. She needed help and the "shrinks" as she called them had given up on her. Perfect timing to come to me!

Janet is an artist with fantastic visualisation ability. Hypnotic regression for her was clear and enlightening. It also taught me a huge amount about recurring life lessons that will continue until you accept and understand the lesson. Within minutes of the regression period, Janet was back in 1107.

Luis   Janet, describe to me what you can see. Is it day or night?

Janet   It is day and it's hot. The sun is at its peak. The sand is burning me right through my sandals. I'm in the desert, next to a pond. I've been washing clothes all day and I'm tired. It's now time to go home.

Luis   What is your name?

Janet   People call me Mishka. Erie calls me Mish.

Luis   Who is Erie?

Janet   Erie is a good-looking boy. We rather fancy each other even though I'm being given to a terrible lord called Moonachie. He wants to marry me, but he is cruel and I am really afraid of him. God, I hate him, I wish my mother would come and take me away from this terrible place.

Luis   Mish, where is this terrible place?

Janet   Like I told you, in the desert. Don't ask me such silly questions. We all live in this desert. Everyone lives here. It's the whole world. I can't believe it all looks so terrible. It's no fun living here. I want to go back to my mother, but she has not come back to fetch me like she promised. I've been living in my aunt's house for the last eleven years. My mother brought me here when I was three. She was beautiful you know? But Anaheim (Later we found out this was her aunt Nancy in this life) says she will probably never come back. The men love her, you know? She has the most beautiful jewellery. I think Anaheim is jealous of my mother. She is stuck with Nahoom, and he is not very nice. Actually, he smells like his camels (Laughs out loud and pointed to the distance).

A School Called Earth

Luis Tell me Mish, what happens next?

Janet Erie is helping me carry the water and the clothes back to Nahoom's house where Anaheim is preparing the food. Erie always helps around the place. He lives with us but he sleeps outside in the tent. I really like him. I wish I could marry him, but he has no money of his own. He doesn't even own a camel. His parents were killed in the big war a few years back. Nahoom and some of the other men warriors killed Erie's parents and now he works for Nahoom. What a shame, such a clever boy working for a man that thinks and smells like a camel, don't you think?

Luis I suppose you are right. Tell me Mish, what happens next.

Janet (Rather disturbed) Listen, Michaelilu, stop calling me Mish, only Erie calls me by that name. To you its Mishka, wings or no wings, ok? (P.S. My clients call me Michaelilu when under regression!)

Luis Sorry, MISHKA, please go on.

Janet Nothing, it's always the same, nothing happens. I wash, carry water (said very proudly), go home, the men eat, then we eat and then we clean up and go to sleep. Like I said, nothing happens, but that's how it is. Everyone else does the same.

Luis Mishka (I won't make the mistake of calling her Mish again), I want you to go to the most significant day of your life. Go to the most significant lesson you learn in that life and tell me what happens.

A School Called Earth

Janet   I'm carrying water again. I'm alone, but I'm so unhappy. Moonachie came to visit last night and he got angry and swore at me because I wouldn't smile at him. He beat Erie because Erie took too long to feed his silly camels. He called me an ugly crow, said no one would ever marry someone as ugly and skinny as me. He said I would be lucky if any man would ever look at me. Uncle is cross because I have now insulted his home. Moonachie is very important to Nahoom and now I have ruined the whole situation. Anaheim says we probably have to move away from here now.

Janet then stopped as fear gripped her. Her breathing accelerated as her whole body went rigid and she spoke very softly. I quickly removed her from the situation and desensitised the event. Mishka now watched the event unfold as if it was a movie.

Janet   Oh my God, it's Moonachie on his huge horse. He's riding straight for me and there is nowhere to hide. Now he is getting off is horse and he is yelling at me again. Stop! Stop hitting me. He has ripped off all my clothes. He is on top of me now. Dear God make him stop. It's all going black, no wait it's all going bright white. Strange? Look down there, there is Moonachie, and there lies a girl. Her throat is cut, looks like she is dead, no wait a minute that's me, am I dead? Michaelilu, what is happening, am I dead?

I covered her in protective white light, and she immediately calmed down and smiled. Hi Michaelilu she said, thanks for being here, you have made it easier for me to go home. Come on Michaelilu, let's hurry, let's go home.

Luis	Tell me what happens next. I know where we are going, but I want you to give me your perspective on your experience. By what name do you go?
Janet	You can call me Hymenia
Luis	Look down at yourself and tell me what you see?
Janet	Purple, rose and yellow, I look like the rainbow, but with more purple and rose.
Luis	Describe to me what is happening next?
Janet	I am floating, there is a pulling. I am floating towards white light. Look, there are some people waiting for me. Here they come. It's Brian (son in this life who was Erie) and Henry (a friend) and Trudy (who was Anaheim). They are so pleased to see me. There a whole lot of them, they're my family, this is such joy. I'm glad to be back.

I left Janet for a while to spend time with her friends and soul family members. It is necessary to give clients a bit of time to re-acquaint themselves in the spirit world before moving on.

Luis	Go on what happens next?
Janet	(Sounding annoyed at my intrusion) It's time to go. One of my guides is here, Ariel. We must go on to be cleansed.

Souls often get taken to a place where earthly trauma is desensitised and they get cleaned of any negative emotions. They shed their earthly bodies but the memories will remain traumatic unless they are treated.

A School Called Earth

Luis   So where are you now?

Janet   I am at the bathhouse. There are many baths here. There are many nurturers here as well. They are going to help me get cleaned-up. They will clear my entire earthly trauma, before I go on to the Council of Elders.

Janet then described the delicate and compassionate cleaning process. By the time she re-emerged, my client's face was gleaming with joy. Her voice had changed and she spoke with authority.

Luis   Sorry to interrupt the fun, Hymenia, but let's move on.

Janet   Well, Michaelilu, as you know it's time for a review. I'm going to the Council of Elders so they can review my past life, well, more like we can review it together.

Luis   Do you go alone and what happens next?

Janet   Michaelilu!? You know that answer, No, Ariel comes with but she will just observe. This is a beautiful place. It is so quiet and peaceful in here. The Council is waiting. Now we are watching my past life. We discuss the meaning and the lesson. Mmm, looks like I need to learn some more tough lessons. I did not cope well with abandonment but I faired well in resolve. Can't wait to test myself again.

Luis   What, you mean you want more?

Janet   Absolutely, I have so much more to learn, but I'll choose a much different life though. Looks like Moonachie will be there again, but next time I'll learn the lesson better.

A School Called Earth

Moonachie was back in Janet's life. He again raped her causing the anxiety she has had to learn to deal with, the very reason she came to see me. However, this time Moonachie, (Kandido was his name in this lifetime), was caught and has been punished by the legal system. A few years ago he died alone and in shame. Karma closed, yet Janet's lessons go on.

I then asked Hymenia and Ariel if we could visit my soul group to get some more answers for this book. What happened next you can read in her letter to me.

Janet came out of the regression more alive than ever before. She has found her purpose in her life and become more aware of the Creator and her soul's connection to all that is. She has found the balance and has once again learnt to love. Relationships are now much easier and she now loves life.

I am blessed to be a part of her friendship circle.

Every morning when you awaken from
your visit to the Spirit world.
Look up at the Sun,
And know you have come back to tackle
the challenge you came here for in the first place.
Then say thank you, to the Creator, for He allowed His
Son/Daughter to experience the tough challenge once again.

CIAO FOR NOW

A School Called Earth

Dear friend.

This book is my philosophy and my truth. The reason I have written this book is so that you can find your own enlightenment. Enlightenment means the path for your own spiritual growth. It is uniquely your own. No other person's enlightenment can totally enlighten you. It will merely provide some guidance as you search for your own purpose and way. Chocolate tastes great, but only once you have tasted it can you comment on my opinion of chocolate. Go out and taste your own. Listen to your soul and to your guides. They will lead the way.

And most importantly, don't forget about the Creator and don't forget to pray and meditate. Trust your soul, it knows the truth and the right way back home.

And, finally, if there is anything you take out of this book and I do mean anything, then it is love. Love your Creator, love your fellow man, love yourself, because unconditional love is why we are all what we are and why we come to this School Called Earth.

Via Con Dios

Janet's Letter To Luis

Dear Luis

I thought of a million things to tell you, but now I don't know where to start.

Firstly let me start by saying, Thank you. Thank you for helping me to answer the questions and sort out my worries, my doubts and my misconceptions. You are a compassionate, sweet, kind soul and you have given of yourself to bless me in ways I cannot begin to explain.

The strangest thing happened after our last consultation. I started to dream like never before. I relived parts of what I saw in the last regression, and I have managed to piece together one or two of the incidents that I couldn't explain.

I am not psychic or gifted in the way that you are by any means. However, meetin g your enormous, frightening, beautiful counterparts made me "feel" something that I feel compelled to share with you. The one thing that I feel very, very strongly about is that the one amazing gift that God has given mankind, is the ability to be loved. Although your task on this earth is an enormous one, please don't forget that God recognises you as a man of flesh and blood and doesn't want you or anyone for that matter to give up on love.

Please don't ever stop doing his wonderful work and please don't shut yourself off from what this strange yet beautiful world can offer you. In order to live in this world you need to be a part of it. The feeling I got was that your soul is so consumed by the sadness of this world, that you don't allow yourself to feel the goodness and love that you offer your clients unconditionally. You cannot keep giving of yourself without replenishing your soul with love and balance.

All your spirit group or whatever those dudes in their robes and masks were, are waiting patiently for you to complete you great task on this earth so that they can learn from your experience. You were the only one in the group not wearing a mask, and I was able to see that emotionally the world is weighing heavily on you. However, your group stands steadfast by you in support.

I wish you all the luck and happiness and all the good stuff in your hypnotherapy venture. Please take care of yourself and be sure to look me up should you ever come down to my part of this world.

You have changed my life and destiny, - Thank-you

Your new friend
Janet